AF519417

THE RIGHTS OF THE CHILD IN INDIA

THE RIGHTS OF THE CHILD IN INDIA

By
JUSTICE RAJKUMAR MANISANA SINGH
Former Chief Justice,
Gauhati High Court
and
Former Chairperson,
Assam Human Rights Commission

AKANSHA PUBLISHING HOUSE
NEW DELHI-110002 (INDIA)

AKANSHA PUBLISHING HOUSE
4649-B/21, Ansari Road
Darya Ganj, New Delhi - 110 002
Email: ektabooks@yahoo.com
Ph. : 23263193 / 9811582579 / 9435116718

The Rights of the Child in India

©Author

First Published 2009

ISBN 978-81-8370-155-6

All rights reserved. No part of this publication may be reproduced or transmitted, in any form or by any means, without prior permission of the author.

Any person who does any unauthorized act in relation to this publication may be liable to criminal prosecution and civil claims for damages.

[The responsibility for the facts stated, conclusions reached etc. is entirely that of the Author. The publisher is not responsible for them, whatsoever.]

PRINTED IN INDIA

Published by **Akansha Publishing House**, New Delhi and Printed at Aryan Enterprises, Delhi.

Dedicated

to

the parent(s)

of

Indians

Contents

Preface

When I was the Chairperson of the Assam Human Rights Commission, I had dealt with a few cases for violation of human rights of the children in the school and within or outside the precincts of the school. Some of the cases were respecting corporal punishment inflicted on students in the school by the school teachers, and other cases were violation of the right to health of the children.

After my retirement, I always remember those cases relating to the rights of the child, especially corporal punishment, which has now been eradicated from the school.

Children are innocent and are at a vulnerable age; children are mentally and physically immature. Because of their physical and mental immaturity, children need special safeguards and care, ie they are to be nurtured, protected and educated. Children are not only the future citizens but also the future of the nation.

The rights of the child provided under relevant laws are to be protected. I hope, this book will help to a certain extent to protect the rights of the child.

RAJKUMAR MANISANA SINGH

CHAPTER 1

Meaning of Child and Convention on the Rights of the Child

CHILD

In the context, child means every human being who has not attained age of 18 unless State or National Laws fix less or more than 18 years. The Children (Pledging of Labour) Act, 1933 provides that "child" means a person who is under the age of 15 years. In the Children Act, 1960, "child" means a boy who has not attained the age of 16 years or a girl who has not attained the age of 18 years. Under the Child Labour (Prohibition and Regulation) Act, 1986, "child" means a person who has not completed his 14th year of age. In the Child Marriage Restraint Act, 1929, "child" means person who, if a male, has not completed twenty-one years of age, and if a female, has not completed eighteen years of age. Therefore, in different context, the National Laws fix less or more than 18 years.

Children are innocent and are at a vulnerable age; children are mentally and physically immature. Because of their physical and mental immaturity, children need special safeguards and care, ie they are to be nurtured, protected and educated. Children are not only the future citizens but also the future of the nation. Education is an investment in the children for harvesting crop of responsible persons of a well-being society.

INTERNATIONAL INSTRUMENTS

International community was concerned for the rights of children that there should be the promotion of separate rights for the children. Situated thus, the following Declarations and Convention were adopted, namely -

Firstly - Geneva Declaration of the Rights of the Child of 1924, adopted on 26 September 1924 by the League of Nations.

Secondly - Declaration of the Rights of the Child of 1959, adopted by the General Assembly of the United Nations on 20 November 1959.

Lastly - Convention on the Rights of the Child of 1989, adopted on 20 November 1989 by the General Assembly of the United Nations (see Appendix II).

The above Declarations and Convention have been a guide to the private and public actions in the interest of children ever since, and the Declarations or the Convention is the moral framework for children's rights today.

HIGHLIGHTS OF THE CONVENTION OF 1989

The Convention on the Rights of the Child of 1989 (hereinafter, the "Convention of 1989") provides, inter alia, as under-

1. Each child enjoys rights set forth in the Convention without discrimination or distinctions of any kind.
2. In all actions concerning children, whether undertaken by courts of law, social welfare institutions, administrative authorities or legislative bodies, the best interests of the child shall be of a primary consideration.
3. Every child has the inherent right to life; and States shall ensure to the maximum extent possible the survival and development of the child.

4. Every child has the right to a name and nationality from birth.
5. Children should not be separated from their parents against their will, except by competent authorities for their well-being in accordance with applicable law and procedures.
6. To facilitate reunification of families by permitting travel into, or out of, their territories.
7. To take all the appropriate legislative, administrative, social and educational measures to protect children from all forms of physical or mental violence, injury or abuse, neglect, including sexual abuse or exploitation.
8. Disabled children shall have the right to special treatment, education and care.
9. The child is entitled to the highest attainable standard of health. States shall ensure that health care is provided to all children, placing emphasis on preventive measures, health, education and reduction of infant mortality.
10. Primary education shall be free and compulsory; school discipline is to be administered in the manner consistent with the child's human dignity. Encourage the development of different forms of secondary education including general and vocational education.
11. Children shall have the right to rest and play and to participate freely in cultural life and artistic activities.
12. Protection of the child from economic exploitation and from performing any work that may interfere with education or be harmful to health and well-being.
13. States shall protect children from the illegal use of drugs and involvement in drug production or trafficking.
14. To make all efforts to eliminate the abduction and trafficking of children.
15. Children involved in infringements of the penal law shall be treated in a way that promotes their sense of dignity and worth and that aims at reintegrating them into society.

The Government of India acceded to the Convention of 1989 on 11 December 1992 after about 3 years of its adoption.

UP-TO-DATE RIGHTS OF THE CHILD

The Convention of 1989 is in the best interest of the child. The Convention provides whatever the freedoms and rights which a child needs and the primary role of the family and parents in the care and protection of children and also the obligation of the State to help them in carrying out those duties.

Although the global perspective on the rights of the child has been recognized in many international instruments, including the International Covenant on Civil and Political Rights, the International Covenant on Economic, Social and Cultural Rights and the Universal Declaration of Human Rights of 1948, **the Convention of 1989** is something special, and it has brought together all the rights of the child described in many International Instruments in one up-to-date.

WORLD CONFERENCE ON HUMAN RIGHTS

The "World Conference on Human Rights" convened at Vienna, Austria, in June 1993 adopted the "Vienna Declaration and Programme of Action" on 25 June 1993. The World Conference on Human Rights, while dealing with the rights of the child, reiterated the principle of "First Call for Children", and, in this respect, underlines the importance of major national and international efforts, especially those of the United Nations Children's Fund, for promoting respect for the rights of the child to survival, protection, development, and participation.

The following are, inter alia, programme of actions under the Vienna Declaration and Programme of Action respecting the rights of the child: —

(1) To take measures to achieve universal ratification of the Convention on the Rights of the Child by 1995;

(2) To place priority on reducing infant and maternal mortality rates, reducing malnutrition and illiteracy rates and providing access to safe drinking-water and to basic education;

(3) To combat actively against exploitation and abuse of children, including by addressing their root causes;

(4) To abolish existing laws and regulations and to remove customs and practices which discriminate against and cause harm to the girl child; and

(5) To study into the means of improving the protection of children in armed conflicts.

The above clearly indicates that international community is very much concerned for the rights of the child prescribed in the Convention of 1989.

THE COMMISSIONS FOR PROTECTION OF CHILD'S RIGHTS ACT, 2005

It is an act made by the Parliament of India to provide for the constitution of a National Commission and State Commissions for Protection of Child Rights and Children's Courts for providing speedy trial of offences against children or of violation of child rights and for matters connected therewith or incidental thereto. Under that Act, "child rights" has been defined to include "the Children's rights adopted in the United Nations convention on the Rights of the Child on 20th November, 1989 and ratified by the Government of India on the 11th December, 1992".

In view of the above, rights prescribed in the Convention on the Rights of the Child (1989) have become a national law. The functions of the National Commission and those of the State Commission have been provided in the Child Rights Act. There shall be Children's Courts for the purpose of providing speedy trial of offences against the Children or of violation of child rights. There shall also be a Special Public Prosecutor for the purpose of conducting cases before Children's Courts.

For the reason stated, violation of the child rights has now become an offence triable by a Special Court.

THE COMMISSIONS FOR PROTECTION OF CHILD RIGHTS (AMENDMENT) ACT, 2006

The Commissions for Protection of Child Rights has been amended by the Amendment Act of 2006 respecting who shall be Chairman of the Selection Committee for the appointment of Chairperson and other members of the National Commission.

CHAPTER 2

Education and Teacher Education

EDUCATION

Many scholars and philosophers have described the word "education" in different ways as if "education" is a word of art in different contexts at different periods. To me, "education" is a technical term and is not a word of art. The concept of education is to train up young and / or old in learning. Whether she or he is old or not, one can learn by or through study, reading, instruction, practice, experience, or being taught. Therefore, "education", in its true sense of the term, is a system of teaching and learning designed to give knowledge and to develop skills, abilities, character, physical fitness, moral standard and mental powers from such training, study, experience, instruction or teaching in the process of teaching and learning.

EDUCATIONAL INSTITUTIONS

Education is generally imparted to the children at educational institution such as school. As regards the "educational institution", it shall not be called or considered as the "educational institution" as such just because it has buildings, chairs, desks, benches, students and teachers; for the having or possessing of the above is not enough, it must have all the basic needs necessary for accomplishment of the full scope of educational instruction, including those things essential for development of mental power, moral standard, physical fitness and skills.

The question, then, is whether the "field of study dealing with how to teach effectively" will come within the ambit and scope of education. The matter relates to the acquisition of knowledge of a subject, viz how to teach or impart knowledge by devoting time and thought. Therefore, acquisition of all knowledge tending to train and develop individual will fall within the meaning of education. In this view of the matter, educational institutions such as colleges or schools of education are now established as field of study dealing with how to teach effectively.

TEACHER EDUCATION

The National Council for Teacher Education Act, 1993 ("the NCTE Act", for short) was enacted by the Parliament to provide for the establishment of a National Council for Teacher Education with a view to achieving planned and co-ordinated development of the teacher education system throughout the country, the regulation and proper maintenance of norms and standards in the teacher education system and for matters connected therewith.

Under the NCTE Act, "'teacher education' means programmes of education, research or training of persons for equipping them to teach at pre-primary, primary, secondary and senior secondary stages in schools, and includes non-formal education, part-time education, adult education and correspondence education"

The definition of "teacher education" prescribed under the NCTE Act consists of two parts. In the first part, the word "means" has been used intending what "teacher education" means. The second part brings within the purview of the "teacher education" certain categories of teaching system respecting non-formal education, part-time education, adult education and correspondence education.

The National Council for Teacher Education (Council) has been constituted by the Central Government in terms of the NCTE Act; and four Regional Committees have been established by the Council, namely the Eastern Regional Committee, the Western Regional Committee, the Northern Regional Committee and the Southern Regional Committee.

TEACHER TRAINING

In this book, the subject is confined mainly to training of persons for equipping them to teach the school children.

At the present day, the establishment of a college or school of education, viz teacher's training institute, shall be governed by the provisions of the NCTE Act. Teacher's training institutes (colleges or schools of education) are to be recognized by the appropriate Regional Committee to enable teacher's training institutes to offer a course or training in teacher education. The "examining body" shall, on receipt of such an order granting recognition, grant affiliation to the institution. The "examining body" has been described in the NCTE Act as:

> "'examining body' means a University, agency or authority to which an institution is affiliated for conducting examinations in teacher education qualifications".

Recognition is one thing and affiliation is another. There is significant difference between the two words "recognition" and "affiliation." In the context, "affiliation" is meant to prepare and present students for public examinations conducted by the "examining body", whereas recognition is for the purpose of enabling a teacher's training institute to offer a course or training in "teacher education" officially or formally, otherwise know as the "recognised institutions".

FUNCTIONS OF THE COUNCIL

The functions of the Council are prescribed in the NCTE Act. On a reading of the NCTE Act, it is clear that the pivotal role of the Council is to shape up teacher education system, including the development of the field of study dealing with how to teach effectively or how to produce qualified teachers, so that the education of the child be directed to meaningful education or valued education. Therefore, it shall be the duty of the Council to take all such steps as it may think fit for ensuring planned and co-ordinated development of the "teacher education". Provisions have been made under the NCTE Act for determination and maintenance of standards for "teacher education" and for the purpose of performing its functions.

QUALIFIED TEACHERS

The teacher's training institutes are meant for training of persons for equipping them to be qualified teachers to teach children in the educational institutions. Children are innocent and are at vulnerable age, in other words, children are mentally and physically immature. Because of their physical and mental immaturity, children need special safeguards and care. Therefore, teachers play important roles in the development of child's career, character, personality, talents, mental and physical abilities, as well as moral, spiritual, cultural or social activities. Situated thus, the teacher needs to be equipped with scientific and technical knowledge and modern teaching methods to impart lessons with the latest techniques to the children. Teachers, as delegates of the parental authority, are the instruments for the preparation of the children for becoming responsible citizens of the free and modern society, or of the nation. In the context, it may be stated that unqualified teachers will be detrimental to the present education system and will also be harmful to the children. Here lies the importance of the qualified teachers.

At this stage, an observation made in a decision of the Supreme Court[1] may be extracted –

> ". . . Though teaching is the last choice in the job market, the role of teacher is central to all process of formal education. The teacher alone could bring out the skills

1. *Andhra Kesari Educational Society* Vs *Director of School Education,* (1989) 1 SCC 392.

and intellectual capabilities of students. He is the "engine" of the educational system. He is the principal instrument in awakening the child to cultural values. He needs to be endowed and energized with needed potential to deliver enlightened services expected of him. His quality should be such as would inspire and motivate into action the benefactor. He must keep himself abreast of ever changing conditions. He is not to perform in a wooden and unimaginative way. He must eliminate fissiparous tendencies and attitude and infuse noble and national idea in younger minds. His involvement in the national integration is more important, indeed indispensable. It is, therefore, needless to state that teachers should be subjected to rigorous training with rigid scrutiny of efficiency. It has greater relevance to the need of the day. The ill-trained or sub-standard teachers would be detrimental to our education system; if not a punishment on our children. The Government and the University must, therefore, take care to see that inadequacy in the training of teachers is not compounded by any extraneous consideration."

The above observation of the Supreme Court has to be noted by all concerned with education.

CHAPTER 3

Child's Right to Education and Child Labourers

FREE AND COMPULSORY EDUCATION

The Convention of 1989 provides, inter alia, for making "primary education compulsory and available free to all". As regards the binding nature of the International Instruments, the general principle is that International Treaties or Conventions do not automatically become part of the National Law. They have to be incorporated into the legal system by appropriate law. But National Courts generally interpret statutes so as to maintain harmony with the rules of the International Law. The National Legislation, even if contrary to International Law, has to be respected. The power to implement treaties belongs exclusively to the Union under the Constitution. However, there are decisions of the apex court that the International Instruments, particularly those to which India is a party, become part of Indian law so long as they are not inconsistent with the Indian law and, therefore, they can well be relied upon and enforced.[1] As was stated, the Government of India acceded to the Convention of 1989 on 11 December 1992. The provisions prescribed in the Convention of 1989 have now incorporated into the legal system of the

---

1. *Prem Shankar Shukla* Vs *Delhi Administration*, AIR 1980 SC 1535, *Sheela Barse* Vs *Secretary, Children's Aid Society*, (1987) 3 SCC 50; *People's Union for Civil Liberties* Vs *Union of India*, (1997) 3 SCC 433; *Apparel Export Promotion Council* Vs *AK Chopra*, (1999) 1 SCC 759.

national law, namely the Commission for Protection of Child Rights Act, 2005.

By the Constitution (Eighty-sixth Amendment) Act of 2002, a new Article, namely Article 21A, was introduced or inserted in the Constitution and Article 45 of the Constitution was amended. The new Article 21A runs as:

> "**Right to education**.—The State shall provide free and compulsory education to all children of the age of six to fourteen years in such manner as the State, may, by law, determine".

After the amendment, Article 45, now, runs:

> "**Provision for early childhood care and education to children below the age of six years**.—The State shall endeavour to provide early childhood care and education for all children until they complete the age of six years".

Before the amendment, Article 45 provided:

> "**Provisions for free and compulsory education for children**.—The State shall endeavour to provide, within a period of ten years from the commencement of this Constitution, for free and compulsory education for all children until they complete the age of fourteen years"

The Article 45, as it stood, directed the State should take steps for free and compulsory education for all children up to the age of fourteen within a period of ten years after the "commencement of the Constitution". The twenty-sixth day of January 1950 has been described in the Constitution as the day of the "commencement of the Constitution", although some of the Articles (sixteen Articles) of the Constitution came into force prior to 26.01.1950, namely on 26.11.1949. However, by force of the Constitution, the expression "commencement of the Constitution" refers to 26.01.50 and not to 26.11.1949. This being the position, 10 years referred to above expired on twenty-fifth January 1960, before introducing or inserting Article 21A relating to the right to education. In this context, it may be mentioned that the Supreme Court has, before the aforesaid amendment of the Constitution, recognized the right to education as a fundamental right by holding that

> "every child/citizen of this country has a right to free education until he completes the age of fourteen".[1]

It may be stated that although the "right to education" was made one of the fundamental rights, nothing is seen practically till date; and Article 21A providing right to free and compulsory education remains only in the statute-book.

CHILD LABOUR

Today, the international community is also very much concerned about the child labour. The Convention of 1989 provides, inter alia, "States Parties recognize the right of the child to be protected from economic exploitation and from performing any work that is likely to be hazardous or interfere with the child's education or to be harmful to the health or physical, mental, spiritual, moral or social development". The expression "State Parties", in the context, means the Country which signed and ratified the Convention (by instrument of ratification) or acceded to the Convention by instrument of accession. As regards the binding nature of the international instruments, it has already been discussed above.

In this context, a report on child labour by UNESCO may be mentioned. The report states that nearly 6% of the children between 5-14/15 years in India are working as labourers in various formal sectors. It has also been reported by the PTI, New Delhi, 31 December 2000, to the effect that "India has 1.35 crore child labourers." At any event, the existence of a number of child-labourers in India in rural and urban cannot be disputed. How to solve it is the problem.

Income is essential for livelihood. Income is also foundation to enjoy many rights guaranteed by the Constitution and also enjoyment of life and its attainments—social, cultural and

1. *Unni Krishnan* Vs *State of Andhra Pradesh*, (1993) 1 SCC 645 (732)

intellectual—without which life cannot be meaningful. Man has, therefore, to work for food and enjoyment of life. But right to employment has not been declared as one of the fundamental rights, perhaps, because of the financial constraints, though the Constitution of India promises socio-economic justice and also to make provisions respecting right to work. In this view of the matter, the "educational planning" is an important factor and when the question of "educational planning" arises the planners have to consider the socio-economic fields for removal of the unemployment problem, including child labourers.

SOME PROVISIONS UNDER THE CONSTITUTION

Article 21 of the Constitution of India provides:

> "No person shall be deprived of his life or personal liberty except according to procedure established by law".

"Right to life" guaranteed by the Constitution has been interpreted to include the right to live with human dignity, free from exploitation. The "right to life" does take in "educational facilities" as the "right to education" is implicit in and flows from the "right to life" guaranteed by the Constitution.[1]

Article 23 of the Constitution of India reads:

> "Traffic in human beings and beggar and other similar forms of forced labour are prohibited and any contravention of this provision shall be an offence punishable in accordance with law".

Article 24 of the Constitution of India runs in the following terms:

> "No child below the age of fourteen years shall be employed to work in any factory or mine or engaged in any other hazardous employment".

---

1. *Bandhua Morcha* Vs *Union of India*, AIR 1984 SC 802.

STATUTE LAW

Many legislations had been made before and after the commencement of the Constitution prohibiting child labour, for example – The Child Labour (Prohibition and Regulation) Act of 1986, which replaced the Employment of Children Act of 1938, Indian Factories Act of 1948, the Mines Act of 1952, the Motor Transport Workers Act of 1951, the Plantation Labour Act of 1951, the Bidi and Cigar Workers Act of 1966, etc.

JUDICIAL PRONOUNCEMENTS

In spite of the Labour Laws mentioned above, the Supreme Court has issued elaborate guidelines and wide-ranging directions in the context of employment and exploitation of children – prohibiting employment of children below the age of fourteen and making arrangement for their education by creating funds and providing employment to the parents or adult member of the family; child labour shall not be engaged in hazardous employment; there shall be child labour rehabilitation welfare fund in which offending employer should deposit Rs. 20,000; and directions as to education, health and nutrition of child labour.[1]

The State should not only identify bonded labourers but also provide for rehabilitation. Failure to do so would constitute a violation of fundamental rights guaranteed by the Constitution and at the same time, grant of financial assistance shall be adequate.[2]

In respect of the public health, improvement of public health is a primary duty of the State. Hence, the court should enforce this duty against the defaulting local authority[3], on

---

1. *MC Mehta* Vs *State of Tamil Nadu*, AIR 1997 SC 699: (1996) 6 SCC 756 and *Bandhua Mukti Morcha* Vs *Union of India*, AIR 1997 SC 2218: (1997) 10 SCC 549. *Bandhua Mukti Morcha*'s case concerns the employment of children in carpet weaving industries in UP.

2. *Bandhua* Vs *Union of India* AIR 1984 SC 802: *Neeraja* Vs *State of MP*, AIR1984 SC 1099 and *Sivaswamy* Vs *State of AP*, AIR 1988 SC 1863.

3. *Ratlam Municipality* Vs *Vardhichand*, AIR 1980 SC 1622

pain or penalty described by law, regardless of financial resources of such authority.

EDUCATION AND CHILD LABOURS

It is, now, well-settled that a child has right to education. In spite of that, if a child is under employment, his right to education shall be deprived of. The provisions of the Constitution referred to above are in the interest of health and strength of children, but in view of our socio-economic realities the Constitution makers could not prohibit the employment of children generally. Although there are labour laws prohibiting the employment of children in certain industries, the child labour cannot be generally be abolished in other sectors or fields.

Child labour is prohibited by statutes and the international instruments, especially the Convention on the Rights of the Child of 1989, and yet millions and millions of children in India are working as labourers either in the hazardous industries or otherwise in the rural and the urban. Therefore, poor people will remain illiterate. As stated, "educational planning" is an important factor and, therefore, planners have to consider the problem of the child labour also.

As to the "educational planning" for the child labourers, the relevant provisions of the Constitution can be pressed into service to make suitable provisions regarding child labourers respecting their education; and the appropriate Government should make appropriate laws for the achievement of the goals of education of children as is provided under the Constitution of India, for instance—making an appropriate law providing that the employer of the child, who does not provide the child for going to school, shall be an 'act' punishable with fine or otherwise, making a provision in the Conduct Rules in the case of a government servant to the effect that such an 'act' amount to misconduct and shall liable to disciplinary action, etc. It is reiterated that the employment of children cannot be generally abolished in India in the present situation and regards has to be made to the decision of the Supreme Court referred to above regarding the making of arrangement for the education of the child labourers by making funds and providing employment to the parents or adult members of the family where there is employment of children below 14 years.

CHAPTER 4

Quality Education (in a Loose Manner)

QUALITY EDUCATION

When the word "quality" is used in relation to education, in particular in higher education which generally means college or university education as opposed to school or high school, it is a misnomer or unsuitable name for the following reasons—

(a) The word "quality" is used in the matter of finished products, works, things, actions, and the like as the meaning of the word "quality" means **"how good or bad something is".**

(b) In business and industry, the word "quality" is used to mean that quality of a particular product or service of a particular company is good enough for customers for a particular situation or purpose. In other words, quality is fitness for **a particular situation or purpose** in the sense that the product or service meets the satisfaction of customers. For example - every product of Sony is satisfactory, my Maruti Car has given me excellent service, computers are now essential in offices, business, industry etc. The above are the reaction of consumers after using the finished products. As regards other finished product or things and actions, the Taj Mahal is the work of a high standard, hydrogen and oxygen make water, and so on. These are said after seeing the Taj Mahal and after making experience.

(c) Education can never by a finished product or thing, for the area or field of education is very wide, i.e. Arts, General Science, Commerce, Medical Science, Engineering Science, etc. In this view of the matter, no one can have just completed his course on all the subjects or disciplines mentioned above.

For the reasons stated the education cannot be a completed product or things and therefore the use the word "quality" in the matter of education is misnomer or unsuitable word.

FREQUENT USE

The word "quality" when it is used in the matter of education it is a misnomer or unsuitable word, as stated. But the expression "quality in education" or "quality education" is a frequently used and is a much debated term, and it is least understood. That apart, the expression "quality in education" or "quality education" is of recent origin, but the concept of it is for valued education which would be useful in the society.

The valued education or meaningful education possesses **characteristic of quality, but not all**. Therefore, it would be appropriate to call the term "quality" when it used in relation to education as "quasi-quality" or "semi-quality", but such expression may not be suitable in the common parlance and, therefore, it may be called quality development or quality assurance, or any phraseology may be used to indicate quality movement or quality development. However, in this book, the expression **"quality"** has been used **in a loose manner in some places**.

CONCEPT OF QUALITY DEVELOPMENT

The concept of "quality development" has arisen by reason of: firstly, competition among the higher educational institutes for good students; and secondly, the consciousness of students or their parents for the value of time and money spent vis-a-vis job-market.

As regards firstly, there is a strong competition amongst the higher educational institutions for good students. Therefore, for attracting students, the institutions are worrying about the performance of the institution, good books or good library, good students (good understandable students) who can perceive the process of teaching and learning towards the movement of quality and quality of teaching (good teachers). It may be stated, substandard teachers are detrimental to the education system, if not a punishment to the students.

As for secondly, the students or their parents are now highly conscious of the value of time and money spent and therefore they are demanding quality of teaching, **employable skills in the job-market,** etc.

There are many educated unemployed youth in this country, including those who secured very good marks in the examination or those who possess high degree of educational qualifications. Many of them are under the impression that, unless education leads to job, it (education) has no meaning; and long years spent in colleges and/or Universities are no longer useful and the certificates or degrees obtained by them are waste papers and, therefore, they deserve to be thrown away if they do not lead to suitable jobs in the end.

The problem of unemployment in India is a serious one. It is also a fact that the use of modern new technology like computer technology in the industries and offices of the government and public and private undertakings has resulted in financial saving through reduction of manpower and time taken. This has certainly affected the employment problem further.

Income is essential for livelihood. Income is also the foundation to enjoy many rights guaranteed by the Constitution, and also enjoyment of life such as social, cultural and intellectual spheres without which life cannot be meaningful. Man has, therefore, to work for food and enjoyment of life. In this view of the matter, the impression of the educated unemployed youth is not without any reason. But right to employment has not been declared as one of the fundamental rights, perhaps, because of the financial constraint though the Constitution of India promises socio-economic justice. This being the position, the education of values, ie the education which will be useful and helpful in life, is required to make the life meaningful.

EDUCATIONAL PLANNING

In view of the above discussion, the "educational planning" is an important factor, and when the question of "educational planning" arises the planners have to consider the socio-economic fields for removal of the unemployment problem. Situated thus, the problems that the planners have to face are not of simple matter.

It is seen that the planners have been keeping pace with the changing socio-economic norms; where the planning of the past does not fit in the present context, the planners are evolving a new planning to satisfy the needs of the fast changing society and keep abreast of the economic development.; and the planners are aware of the fact that planning cannot be static. But the answer to the questions as to why education cannot be taken beyond a job, and as to why education cannot lead to a job are left at the wisdom of the educational planners.

PRE-INDEPENDENCE EDUCATION

It may be stated that the education which was received before independence did somehow serve to create in the minds of people a sense of security of/for employment. It is just a passing reference; and it is not suggested that everything was well in that system of education. The system of education of those days was mostly for the requirement of the Rulers of the day. However, today all kinds of people (cultured, uncultured, educated, uneducated, political, non-political) say that everything is wrong in the present education system and the system of education is of low or poor quality. This may not be wholly true but attempt has to be made by the planner to achieve the goals and ideals of quality development or useful education to achieve the Constitutional guarantees.

CONSTITUTIONAL IMPLICATION

Education has its legal and Constitutional implication in India. After the Constitution (Forty-second Amendment) Act of 1976, barring the subjects covered by Entries 63 to 65 of Union List (List I), the residue of education has been under Concurrent List (List III). Entry No 66 of the Union List (List I) provides: "Co-ordination and determination of standards in institutions for higher education or research and scientific and technical institutions". Therefore the Central Government is responsible for, inter alia, standards in institutions for higher education.

Section 12 of the University Grants Commission Act of 1956 has provided :

> "It shall be the general duty of the Commission to take, in consultation within Universities or other bodies concerned, all such steps as it may think fit for the promotion and co-ordination of Universities, education and for the determination and maintenance of standards of teaching, examination and research in Universities . . . ".

Under section 2(f) of the UGC Act, University includes

> "any such institution as may, in consultation with University concerned, be recognised by the Commission in accordance with the regulation made in this behalf under this Act."

In terms of the provision under section 12 referred to above, the UGC established the National Assessment and Accreditation Council (the NAAC, for short) at Bangalore on 16.09.94 as per the National Policy on Education. The NAAC is now quality development agency for higher education in India for colleges and universities. At present the NAAC is the only responsible authority in India for quality evaluation for colleges and universities, other than professional education.

QUALITY IN EDUCATIONAL MATTER

Many writers have expressed the meaning of quality in the matter of education. One of the meanings which has given me an impression is the one defined by Sir John Daniel, President and CEO, Commonwealth of Learning. He has said: " I define quality simply as 'fitness for purpose at minimum cost to society' ". Be that as it may, if I have to define quality in higher education, I define as " the educational process which makes students suitable for something or some body"

FACE-TO-FACE EDUCATION

A mention may be made here that many countries are debating whether the colleges or universities (face-to-face) education are useful for providing the education and training which the students need in the present society. Therefore, distance education (learning) and e-learning mode have, perhaps, come up.

CHAPTER 5

Human Rights Education

KNOWLEDGE OF HUMAN RIGHTS

Teachers of the school children should also be educated in human rights, especially the right of the child. The Convention of 1989 provides that the education of the child shall be directed, inter alia, to the development of respect for human rights and fundamental freedoms. And the Convention of 1989 is for the promotion of separate rights for the children providing whatever the freedoms and rights which a child needs. It may be stated here that India not only acceded to the Convention of 1989 but also the Convention of 1989 has now become a part of the Indian law, as stated. Unless the teacher is aware of the human rights, it may not be possible to direct to the development of respect for human rights to the young students. Therefore, teachers teaching children in school should have the knowledge of the human rights. The teachers also must be made aware of the rights of the child in school and within or outside the precincts of the school so that the teacher may treat the school children in accordance with the rights of the child.

RIGHTS OF THE CHILD

There are many rights of the child prescribed by the Constitution and International Instruments, especially the Convention of 1989. A few rights of the child under the Convention of 1989 may be mentioned here, namely – right to education, protections from all forms of physical or mental violence, injury or abuse; entitlement to the highest attainable standard of health; school discipline is to be administered in the manner consistent with child's human dignity; right to rest and play; and protection from any work that may interfere with or may be harmful to health and well-being. Under the Constitution, varieties of rights of the child are guaranteed and are protected. Three of them are right to education, right to health and right against cruelty (physical and mental violence). Out of many rights prescribed, as stated, violation of a few rights of the child are prominently noticed in the educational institutions.

VIOLATION OF HUMAN RIGHTS

As was stated, education of the child should be directed, inter alia, to the development of the respect for human rights and the Constitution provides protection of the rights of the child, but many teachers in various schools in India, instead of protecting the right of the child, violate rights of the child. In this context, what has been stated in the judgment of the Delhi High Court[1] is extracted as under:

"16. Some of the reported incidents are given below for illustrating the point: –

a) A child was beaten and kicked by the teacher for stepping out of the classroom to have a sip of water to control his hiccups.

b) A boy was slapped for a small mistake which caused perforation in his eardrum for which he had to undergo surgery.

c) A boy succumbed to the injuries inflicted by his principal. He was the only child of his parents.

d) Recently, a small girl in school was given a roller blow by the teacher, which caused grave injury on her head. This punishment was meted out to her

---

1. *Parents Forum for Meaningful Education* Vs *Union of India*, AIR 2001 Delhi 212

because she was found peeping into the classroom from outside to look at her elder brother.

The last incident reflects that we have carried inhuman practices even into the new millennium. The list of such incidents is unending.

17. According to the UNICEF's report titled "The State of the World's Children 99", 40 million children dropped out of schools before reaching class V due to substandard learning situations.

18. Studies have shown that spanking of children result in undesirable effects. They become withdrawn and exhibit anti-social behaviour. Children who are ruled by the rod in school may acquire disdain and hatred for their teachers. Beating affects their concentration in studies and leads to development of fear psychosis towards learning. Fear of corporal punishment discourages regular attendance at schools and increases drop out rate. This obviously hampers and obstructs education and affects their right to education, which is a fundamental right flowing from Article 21..."

The decision of the Delhi High Court amply supports the fact of violation of rights of the child by the teachers. This case of the Delhi High Court is further discussed in another Chapter. The above referred to case is about the corporal punishment, which is unconstitutional being in violation of the rights of the child. There are also reports that school children are employed by the teachers for performing work which will be harmful to the health and well-being; and that the right to health of the children in school are not looked after. These also show that teachers of the school children are required to be educated in human rights, especially the rights of the child, as a subject of the practical importance for the protection of the rights of the school children within or outside the precincts of the educational institutions. The human right education shall certainly help to the production of qualified teachers; that also will be highly beneficial to the teachers—not only as the teacher but also as a citizen of India. This may possibly be done by prescribing a course on human rights and the rights of the child in the teacher education system or programme.

AMENDMENT OF NATIONAL POLICY ON EDUCATION

As stated, the Government of India acceded to the Convention of 1989 on 11th December 1992. Before the Government of India acceding to the Convention of 1989, the National Policy on Education was amended to a certain extent. After modification of the National Policy on Education in 1992, corporal punishment has been eradicated from the school.

CHAPTER 6

Human Rights and Protection of Human Rights

HUMAN RIGHTS

As stated, teachers of the school children are to be educated in human rights and rights of the child. The question, then, is what the "human rights" means.

Rights of man are not the only rights those created by man such as laws made by the legislators (legislative body), customs and usages having the force of law; beyond those rights created by man, there lies another idea or concept of rights of man, otherwise known as the "natural rights" originated from the nature, that is to say, those rights originated from nature are called the "natural rights", for example – natural right to the flow of light and air, natural right to the purity of air, natural rights in water of stream or river, etc. Those natural rights are nothing but human rights. Therefore, human rights are natural rights spring from human itself and are the rights which are inherent in human beings. Some called human rights as the "birth right". They are not acquired, nor transferred nor extinguished. Therefore, human rights differ from those man made rights, which can be extinguished or acquired or transferred, as the case may be.

Out of the natural rights or human rights, those which are fundamental or principal rights (for instance – right to life, liberty, equality and dignity of individual) are commonly called as the "basic human rights" or "fundamental human rights". But what are the basic human rights cannot be listed exhaustively till date.

INTERNATIONAL PROTECTION OF HUMAN RIGHTS

It has a long history. There has been a growing concern about the protection of human rights, however, the International Legal Protection of the Rights and Freedoms of the individual are in large measure a post-1945 development (after the end of World War II).

Post-1945 developments have produced a substantial number of treaty instruments. The Universal Declaration of Human Rights was adopted by the General Assembly of the United Nations on 10 December 1948 (see Appendix-I); and the 10th December is known as the "Human Rights Day" later on. It was mainly for the purpose of the International Protection of Human Rights. However, it was not a legally binding instrument, for the international community has no legislative body (Legislature). That apart, the rights included therein have only limited legal substance in the International Law. In that view of the matter, the Universal Declaration of Human Rights has been followed by several International Conventions of which most significant are -

1. **The International Covenant on Economic, Social and Cultural Rights; and**
2. **The International Covenant on Civil and Political Rights.**

They were adopted by the General Assembly on 16 December 1966, and India is a party to the two Covenants.

None of the International Instruments specifically specifies/specify or lists/list what is/are the human rights which is/are to be protected or is/are intended to be protected. In spite of that the basic human rights to be protected are rights to life, liberty, equality and dignity of the individual. It may be stated that human rights and the protection of the human rights have been gradually growing up or developing, and the following human rights are, now, recognized or specified as the fundamental or basic human rights under the Universal Declaration of Human Rights and other International Conventions for protection, preservation and promotion —

1. Right to life,
2. Right to equality
3. Freedom from torture, inhuman or degrading treatment or punishment,
4. Freedom from slavery and servitude,
5. Right to liberty and security of a person,
6. Right to fair and speedy trial,
7. Right to private and family life,
8. Freedom of thoughts, conscience and religion,
9. Right to marry and find a family,
10. Freedom of expression,
11. Right of assembly and association,
12. Freedom of movement,
13. Right to property,
14. Right to education,
15. Right to free elections,
16. Right to economic and social provision; and
17. Collective Human Right (right of self-determination, etc.)

The list of rights and liberties is not a closed one as the dimensions of the human rights have widened because of the changing social realities and emerging trends in nature of crime and violence.

DOMESTIC LEVEL PROTECTION OF HUMAN RIGHTS

Almost all the States (Countries) with written Constitution have embodied some protection of the principal rights and liberties in their Constitution within the framework of the Constitution.

As for India, the fundamental rights contained in Part III of the Constitution represent basic human rights possessed by every human body. Language recorded in Part III of the Constitution shows that it is the duty of, or an obligation imposed on, the State and its public functionaries (instrumentalities and agencies) to promote, protect and preserve human rights, as well as duty to prevent violation of human rights. However, the Supreme Court has, in Bodhisttwa Gautam vs Subbra Chakraborty, AIR 1996 SC 922: (1996) 1 SCC 490, held that fundamental rights can be enforced even against the private bodies and individuals.

Now, coming to the constitutional provision relating to the protection of Basic Human Rights or Fundamental Rights, the Constitution stipulates the enforcement of the Fundamental Rights when there is violation of basic human rights or fundamental rights or when there is an apprehension of violation of Fundamental Rights by the Supreme Court of India or the High Courts in India.

In addition to the Constitutional provisions for protection of human rights, the **Protection of Human Rights Act of 1993** was enacted (see Appendix III); for, although India is a party to the International Covenants on Civil and Political Rights and the International Covenant on Economic, Social and Cultural Rights adopted by the General Assembly of the United Nations on the 16th of December, 1986 and the human rights embodied in the aforesaid Covenants stand substantially protected by the Constitution, there has been growing concern in the country and abroad about the issues relating to human rights and wide-ranging discussions were held at various for such as Chief Ministers Conference on Human Rights, seminars organized in various parts of the country and meetings with leaders of various political parties.

Taking into account the views expressed in those discussions and having regard to the growing concern in the country and abroad, changing social realities and the emerging trends in the nature of crime and violence, the Human Rights Act was enacted for the better protection of human rights and for matters connected therewith or incidental thereto.

PROTECTION OF HUMAN RIGHTS ACT

Under the Protection Human Rights Act of 1993, the National Human Rights Commission has been constituted, and some States of India have also constituted State Human Rights Commissions. The functions and powers of the National Human Rights Commission and the State Human Rights Commissions have been prescribed in the Human Rights Act. One of the main functions is to enquire into the complaint of violation of human rights or abetment thereof, or negligence in the prevention of such violation, by a public servant. There is also provision in the Human Rights Act for the establishment Human Rights Courts for the purpose of providing speedy trial of offences arising out of violation of human rights. The National Human Rights Commission, the State Human Rights Commissions and the Human Rights Courts are additional fora for better protection of human rights in addition to the Supreme Court and the High Courts.

Under the Human Rights Act, "human rights" means the rights relating to life, liberty, equality and dignity of the individual guaranteed by the Constitution or embodied in the International Covenants and enforceable by the Courts in India. Out of a number of existing basic human rights or fundamental rights, only a limited number of rights have been provided in the Human Rights Act, namely the rights relating to life, liberty, equality and dignity of the individual guaranteed by the Constitution or embodied in the International Covenants and enforceable by the Courts in India.

As regards the rights guaranteed by the Constitution, "rights to life and liberty" provided in the Human Rights Act are referable to Article 21 of the Constitution, which provides for "protection of life and liberties"; and that "right to dignity of the individual" (right to live with human dignity) flows from Article 21. The "right to equality" stipulated in the Human Rights Act is relatable to Article 14 of the Constitution which states "equality before law". Therefore, in view of the use of the expression "guaranteed by the Constitution", only those Fundamental Rights or Basic Human Rights guaranteed by the Constitution under Articles 14 and 21 are provided in the

Human Rights Act, and not all the Fundamental Rights guaranteed by the Constitution.

In respect of the "International Covenants" mentioned in the Human Rights Act, "International Covenants" means the International Covenant on Civil and Political Rights and the International Covenant on Economic, Social and Cultural Rights adopted by the General Assembly of the United Nations on 16th December, 1966. As stated, India is a party to the two International Covenants. On a reading of the two International Covenants together with the Constitution, it appears that those human rights embodied in the two International Covenants are substantially protected by the Constitution. However, whether or not those fundamental human rights stipulated in the two International Covenants other than those protected by the Constitution can be enforced by the Courts in India cannot be put in a strait-jacket, it will depend upon the facts of each case considering the jurisdiction of the Supreme Court, the High Courts, the Human Rights Commissions and the Human Rights Courts.

DEVELOPMENT OF HUMAN RIGHTS

Human rights and the protection of human rights have gradually developed and are developing in India. In the development process, the Court has taken an important role, for example – the horizon of the "right to life" and "personal liberty" guaranteed by the Constitution under Article 21 has been expanded in different directions by the judicial pronouncements to the extent undreamed of by the founding fathers of the Constitution, or by the judges who gave it initial gloss; and, today, "right to life" guaranteed by the Constitution means something more than the survival of animal existence; it will include all those aspects of life, which go to make a man's life meaningful, complete, and worth living.

It may be stated that it was once thought that judges do not make laws; they only interpret. But, at present, this notion has been discarded everywhere. Every new decision on every new situation is development of law. Law is not static, nor does it stand still. It moves continually to keep pace with the changing society. Where the law of the past does not fit in the present context, the Court evolves a new law. Law is growing to satisfy the need of the fast changing society. Therefore, "law" is a social machinery; and as a social machinery the law requires to remove any imbalance and to further progress serving all the needs of the Socialist Secular Democratic Republic under the rule of law. Considering this situation along with the provisions of the Directive Principles of State Policy enumerated under Part IV of the Constitution, the horizon of the "right to life" has been expanding.

About the Directive Principles of State Policy, the principles therein laid down are nevertheless fundamental in the governance of the country and it shall be the duty of the State to apply these principles in making laws. The opportunities and facilities provided under the Chapter on Directive Principles should be provided to the people. This being the situation, the Directive Principles are the Commands of the Constitution to the Legislature and Executive. Following the Commands, a large number of social legislations, rules and orders have been made by the competent authority for the welfare of the people in India; for instance – rights to rest and leisure by reduction of working day or hour, annual vacation with full pay for workers and employees, maternity and paternity leave, etc. That apart, the Directive Principles are taken into consideration in giving effect to the fundamental rights. To illustrate it, the right to live with human dignity derives its breadth from Directive Principles of State Policy. Therefore, Directive Principles have been elevated to Inalienable Fundamental Human Rights.

It may further be stated that Chapters on Fundamental Rights and Directive Principles of State Policy under the Constitution are integral part of the Constitution, but the Fundamental Rights guaranteed by the Constitution can be enforced in the Court of Law, whereas the Directive Principles cannot be enforced in the Court of Law as the Constitution itself prohibits the enforcement of the provisions of the Directive Principles. However, it does not mean that Directive Principles are less important than, or less inferior to, the

Fundamental Rights; for the directive principle are Inalienable Fundamental Human Rights, as stated.

It has been stated that the horizon of the "right to life" has been expanded by the judicial pronouncements. At the present time, "right to life" includes the following rights:

(1) right to live with human dignity;

(2) right to education;

(3) right against cruelty, physical or mental violence;

(4) right to health;

(5) right to healthy environment (which includes right to pollution free air, right to potable water and protection against hazardous industries);

(6) right to access to road;

(7) right to reasonable accommodation (right to shelter);

(8) right to privacy;

(9) right to livelihood (as distinguished from right to work);

(10) Right to access to road;

(11) right to immediate aid to starvation death;

(12) right to removal of stench and stink caused by open drain and public excretion, and host of other rights.

But the "right to die" and "right to work" are not included within the meaning of "right to life". However, "right to work" can be claimed after employment under Article 21.

This is how the human rights and protection of human rights have been developing in India. It would further develop more because of the changing social realities and emerging trends in nature of crime and violence.

CHAPTER 7

Discipline and Health Care

Provisions under the Convention of 1989

The relevant provisions of the Convention of 1989 are set out below –

ARTICLE 19

"States Parties shall take all appropriate legislative, administrative, social and educational measures to protect the child from all forms of physical or mental violence, injury or abuse, neglect or negligent treatment, maltreatment or exploitation, including sexual abuse, while in the care of parent(s), legal guardian(s) or any other person who has the care of the child".

ARTICLE 24

"States Parties recognize the right of the child to the enjoyment of the highest attainable standard of health and to facilities for the treatment of illness and rehabilitation of health. States parties shall strive to ensure that no child is deprived of his or her right of access to such health care services".

ARTICLE 28

"States Parties shall take all appropriate measures to ensure that school discipline is administered in a manner consistent with the child's human dignity and in conformity with the present Convention".

ARTICLE 29

"States Parties agree that the education of the child shall be directed to:

(a) The development of respect for human rights and fundamental freedoms, and for the principles enshrined in the Charter of the United Nations:

(b) The preparation of the child for responsible life in a free society, in the spirit of understanding, peace, tolerance, equality of the sexes, and friendship among all peoples, ethnic, national and religious groups and persons of indigenous origin.".

ARTICLE 31

"States Parties recognize the right of the child to rest and leisure, to engage in play and recreational activities appropriate to the age of the child and to participate freely in cultural life and the arts".

"States Parties shall respect and promote the right of the child to participate fully in cultural and artistic life and shall encourage the provision of appropriate and equal opportunities for cultural, artistic, recreational and leisurely activity".

ARTICLE 37

"State Parties shall ensure that:

a) No child shall be subjected to torture or other cruel, inhuman or degrading treatment or punishment. Neither capital punishment nor life imprisonment without possibility of release shall be imposed for the offences committed by persons below eighteen years of age.

b) No child shall be deprived of his or her liberty unlawfully or arbitrarily...".

As stated, the expression "State Parties", in the context, means the Country which signed and ratified the Convention of 1989 (by instrument of ratification) or acceded to the Convention by instrument of accession. India acceded to the Convention and, therefore, India is one of the " States Parties". That apart the provisions of the rights of the child under the Convention of 1989 have become a part of the Indian law, by virtue of the Commissions for Protection of Child's Right Act, 2005.

UNDER THE CONSTITUTION

As was stated, the horizon of the "right to life" guaranteed by the Constitution has been expanded by judicial pronouncements to the extent undreamed of by the founding fathers of the Constitution, or by the judges who gave it initial gloss, and the "right to life" includes, inter alia, the following rights –

1. The right to live with human dignity;
2. The right to education;
3. The right against cruelty, physical or mental violence; and
4. The right to health.

All these rights are available to the child and he cannot be deprived of the same because she or he remains as a human being notwithstanding his or her tender age.

Even the animals are protected against cruelty. Cruelty to animals is punishable under Section 11 of the Prevention of Cruelty to Animals Act, 1960. It is not improper at this point to take notice of the fact that the child has been beaten or slapped or kicked by the teacher for his misbehaviour in the class. Boys succumbed to the injuries inflicted by the teachers. It may be mentioned here that in a case where police officers had beaten up a lady tenant and her minor son, who succumbed to his injuries. The mother was held entitled to compensation against the Delhi Administration[1] for deprivation of the right to life and personal liberties.

1. *Saheli* Vs *Commissioner of Police*, AIR 1990, SC 513

DISCIPLINE

There was a general notion that a schoolmaster had the power to inflict moderate and reasonable corporal punishment for correcting the child. The proverb, *"spare the rod and spoil the child"*, may also be recalled. This moral rule was also there in England. In England, the teacher's right is regarded as a delegation of the parent's rights. As delegate of the parental authority, a head-teacher and a responsible assistant teacher have the right to inflict moderate and reasonable corporal punishment, using a proper instrument. A cane is a proper instrument for girls as well as boys. The school regulations permitted only use of birch rod or cane. If, however, the punishment administered does not satisfy these criteria, the corporal punishment is unlawful and the teacher is liable in criminal proceedings and is also liable to a civil action for damages. In respect of unlawful corporal punishment, reported cases – death caused by excessive beating: the teacher convicted for manslaughter, teacher liable in damages where impairment of the pupil's hearing resulted from moderate blow on head, etc. The power to punish is not only confined to punishing for acts done within the precincts of the school but also outside the school compound such as acts done on way to school and smoking in street in breach of school rules after having returned home at end of school day. (See *Halsbury's Laws of England, 4th Edition, Para 67.)*

The above has now gone a sea change. The Convention of 1989 provides, inter alia, that measures to be taken to protect the child from all forms of physical and mental violence, and that school discipline is administered in a manner consistent with the child's human dignity, and that no child shall be subjected to torture or other cruel, inhuman or degrading treatment or punishment. As stated, the Constitution protects the right of the child against cruelty—physical and mental violence.

It has been already stated that the Government of India acceded to the Convention on 11 December 1992. Before acceding to the Convention, the Government of India modified the National Policy on Education in 1992. After modification,

Para 5.6 of the National Policy on Education provides, inter alia, that corporal punishment will be firmly excluded from the educational system, that is to say – the corporal punishment is to be eradicated from schools.

Today, corporal punishment cannot be inflicted on a child in the educational institution while administering school discipline. In a case arising out of the Delhi School Education Rules (framed under the Delhi School Education Act 1973), where one of the rules (rule 37) provides forms of disciplinary measures, including corporal punishment. A Division Bench of the Delhi High Court[1] quashed the Rule providing corporal punishment, after taking into consideration of the above provisions of the convention of 1989 and the relevant provisions of the Constitution referred to above.

HEALTH CARE

"Health Care" has been used in the sense of the service of a doctor who will be responsible for looking after the health of school children. As was stated, "right to life" provided under the Constitution of India includes "right to health"; and the Constitution provides for protection of the health and strength of the children of tender age . The Convention of 1989 on the Rights of the Child speaks about the right of the child to health; and also the right of the child to rest and leisure, and to engage in play and recreation activities appropriate to the age of the child. The right to rest and leisure, and to engage in play and recreation activities are connected with health of the children directly or indirectly.

For securing health and strength of the tender age of the school children, the authority of a school should appoint one doctor (male or female, as the case may be, according to single-sex school) on such part-time or full time basis as may be necessary for looking after the health of the school children. The school authority shall also have to make provisions for recreational facilities for the school children, as well as for rest and leisure for the school children, for example - places or equipment for the school children to use to enjoy themselves.

1. *Parents Forum for Meaningful Education* Vs *Union of India,* AIR 2001 Delhi 212

CHAPTER 8

Child's Right to Play, etc.

CHILD'S RIGHT TO PLAY

Article 31 of the Convention on the rights of the Child of 1989 provides:

> **"State Parties recognize the right of the child to rest and leisure, to engage in play and recreational activities appropriate to the age of the child and to participate freely in cultural life and the arts".**

Therefore, a State Party to the Convention has an obligation to make provision or arrangements for the children for the enjoyments of their above rights. On a reading of the Convention of 1989, it appears that the Convention also provides role of the parents, guardians or any other person who has the care of the children in encouraging the children in the enjoyment of their above rights. It has been stated that India acceded to the Convention of 1989 on 11 December 1992 and, therefore, India is a State Party to the Convention. That apart, the rights of the child described in the Convention of 1989 has become a part of the Indian law, as stated. Situated thus, the Government of India or the State Government, as the case may be, has also an obligation to make provision or arrangements for the children for the enjoyment of their rights described above. In fact, the Government of India modified, before acceding to the Convention, the National Policy on Education to a certain extent in tune with some parts of the Convention, as stated.

PLAY AND RECREATION

When the children play, they do that things they enjoy, for example—some children enjoy when they play hide-and-seek, some other children are amused by playing of chasing each other and so on. Children at play make happy shouts or sounds of laughing. The happy shouts or laughing sounds of children at play reveal or show that children are enjoying and feeling pleasure. Therefore, the children do for pleasure, enjoyment or amusement. There are different varieties of play. Play may be in the form of a programme which aims to teach road safety, cleanliness, etc through play. In other words, there are advantages of learning through play. Play also connotes to take part in a game or sport, and the corollary of that is that a game or sport is a form of play according to fixed or agreed rules.

Recreation is means of refreshing, relaxing or entertaining oneself after work, that is to say — activities that one does for pleasure, enjoyment or amusement are recreational activities such as hobby, pastime or leisure. Therefore, a child's favorite recreational activities would be different from child to child; the favorite recreational activities of a child would be something that the child desires to do for her or his pleasure, enjoyment or amusement; and the recreational facilities would be places or equipment for the children to use to enjoy themselves.

Rest, leisure, recreation activities, play and taking part in sports or games are all for pleasure, enjoyment or amusement; and pleasure, enjoyment or amusement makes the development sound mind or mental power. However, sports or games involving physical activities may differ from the activities of rest or leisure to a certain extent.

SPORT

Sport means something one does competitive and physical activities for pleasure, enjoyment, amusement or recreation. Therefore, the main essentials of sport are competitive and physical activities, and some time luck. Competitive activity, in the context, is in the sense of trying to win by making a good and practical decision in a given situation; and physical activities, in the context, would mean movement of body skillfully in order to achieve success or to win. Therefore, sport involves physical skills and intellectual acumen (ability to think quickly and make a good decision or judgment), and some time luck. It may be stated that certain games does not involve physical activities.

Sport is an integral part of the human nature, for history tells that sport and gaming activities are used as means to socialize, to display skills and power, and to entertain and make excitement and pleasure. In the context, " to socialize" means to spend time with other people in a friendly way. In the modern time, there are many professional sports or games such as tennis, football, cricket and so forth. The professional players display their skills and powers and make entertainment, excitement and pleasure to audience either in the play area or on TV.

REQUIREMENT OF PLAY OR SPORT

Play or game or sport is very important to a child's development. But the children are not necessarily required to play sports or games for becoming professional sport persons as every one may not become a professional player. Children are to play or take part in sports or games mainly or primarily for purpose of their pleasure, enjoyment or amusement because such playing or taking part in sport or game makes the development of sound mind (or mental power), sound body (sound health), skills and intelligence because of what have been stated above.

As was stated, it is the right of the child to rest and leisure, and to engage in play and recreational activities appropriate to the age of the child. One of the reasons is, perhaps, the above rights of the children are for the welfare (in its widest sense) of the child and they are necessary in the present education system as they make development of skills, intelligence, mental power and physical fitness; for education means a system of teaching and learning designed to give knowledge and to develop skills, abilities, character, physical fitness, moral standard and mental power from such training, study, experience, instruction, or teaching in the process of teaching and learning, as stated. In some schools, athletics or sports or games are prescribed as school subject or lesson.

ROLE OF THE GOVERNMENT AND EDUCATION INSTITUTIONS

As stated, the India Government or the State Government, as the case may be, has an obligation to provide facilities, places and equipment or make provision or arrangements for the children in order that the children should enjoy their rights to rest and leisure, and to engage in play and recreational activities. This is concerned for all the children in the country, whether she or he goes to school or not.

As regards the children in the educational institutions (hereinafter as the "schoolchildren"), the responsibility of the State respecting the above rights of the children is shared with the State-recognized private educational institutions for the following reasons. Every citizen has a "right to education" under the Constitution. Therefore, the State is under an obligation to establish educational institutions to enable the citizens to enjoy their "rights to education". But the State is unable to provide sufficient number of educational institutions; it may be because of the limits of its economic capacity or otherwise. Therefore, the State is discharging its obligation through State-owned or State-recognized private educational institutions by granting permission to establish educational institutions; and when the State Government grants reorganization to the private educational institutions, it creates an agency to fulfill obligation of the State Government under the Constitution, namely obligation to establish educational institution. Therefore, the authorities of the State-recognized private educational institutions step into the shoes of the State Government in the matter of the welfare of the schoolchildren, in order words, the authorities of the State-recognized private educational institutions shall have charge of those responsibilities of the State respecting welfare of the schoolchildren in the educational institutions. However, it is noticed that some State-recognized private educational institutions are converted into **"teaching shops"** by charging high fees for various things in consideration of admission to the private educational institutions, which is unconstitutional. (See also **Unni Krishnan's case, supra**). Be that as it may, when the State Government grants reorganization to the private educational institutions, the authorities of the State-recognized private educational institutions shall have charge of those responsibilities of the State respecting welfare of the schoolchildren in the educational institutions.

SUMMING-UP

For the State-owned educational institutions, the State Government has to make provision for the schoolchildren to enable them to enjoy their rights to rest and leisure, and to engage in play and recreational activities. As stated, authorities of State-recognized private educational institutions shall have charge of those responsibilities of the State respecting welfare of the schoolchildren. Therefore, the authority of a State-recognized private educational institution shall have to make provision or arrangements for the schoolchildren to enable them to enjoy their rights to rest and leisure, and to engage in play and recreational activities, which are necessary in the present educational system. It has been stated that play connotes to take part in games or sports, and the recreational facilities would be places or equipment for the schoolchildren to use to enjoy themselves appropriate to the age of the child. The parents or guardians also should encourage the schoolchildren in the enjoyment of their rights to rest and leisure, and to engage in play and recreational activities, as stated.

APPENDIX I

UNIVERSAL DECLARATION OF HUMAN RIGHTS

(Adopted by the General Assembly of the United Nations on 10 December 1948)

PREAMBLE

Whereas recognition of the inherent dignity and of the equal and inalienable rights of all members of the human family is the foundation of freedom, justice and peace in the world,

Whereas disregard and contempt for human rights have resulted in barbarous acts which have outraged the conscience of mankind, and the advent of a world in which human beings shall enjoy freedom of speech and belief and freedom from fear and want has been proclaimed as the highest aspiration of the common people,

Whereas it is essential, if man is not to be compelled to have recourse, as a last resort, to rebellion against tyranny and oppression, that human rights should be protected by the rule of law,

Whereas it is essential to promote the development of friendly relations between nations,

Whereas the peoples of the United Nations have in the Charter reaffirmed their faith in fundamental human rights, in the dignity and worth of the human person and in the equal rights of men and women and have determined to promote social progress and better standards of life in larger freedom,

Whereas Member States have pledged themselves to achieve, in co-operation with the United Nations, the promotion of universal respect for and observance of human rights and fundamental freedoms,

Whereas a common understanding of these rights and freedoms is of the greatest importance for the full realization of this pledge,

Now, therefore*, THE GENERAL ASSEMBLY *proclaims

THIS UNIVERSAL DECLARATION OF HUMAN RIGHTS as a common standard of achievement for all peoples and all nations, to the end that every individual and every organ of society, keeping this Declaration constantly in mind, shall strive by teaching and education to promote respect for these rights and freedoms and by progressive measures, national and international, to secure their universal and effective recognition and observance, both among the peoples of Member States themselves and among the peoples of territories under their jurisdiction.

Article 1

All human beings are born free and equal in dignity and rights. They are endowed with reason and conscience and should act towards one another in a spirit of brotherhood.

Article 2

Everyone is entitled to all the rights and freedoms set forth in this Declaration, without distinction of any kind, such as race, colour, sex, language, religion, political or other opinion, national or social origin, property, birth or other status.

Furthermore, no distinction shall be made on the basis of the political, jurisdictional or international status of the country or territory to which a person belongs, whether it be independent, trust, non-self-governing or under any other limitation of sovereignty.

Article 3

Everyone has the right to life, liberty and security of person.

Article 4

No one shall be held in slavery or servitude; slavery and the slave trade shall be prohibited in all their forms.

Article 5

No one shall be subjected to torture or to cruel, inhuman or degrading treatment or punishment.

Article 6

Everyone has the right to recognition everywhere as a person before the law.

Article 7

All are equal before the law and are entitled without any discrimination to equal protection of the law. All are entitled to equal protection against any discrimination in violation of this Declaration and against any incitement to such discrimination.

Article 8

Everyone has the right to an effective remedy by the competent national tribunals for acts violating the fundamental rights granted him by the constitution or by law.

Article 9

No one shall be subjected to arbitrary arrest, detention or exile.

Article 10

Everyone is entitled in full equality to a fair and public hearing by an independent and impartial tribunal, in the determination of his rights and obligations and of any criminal charge against him.

Article 11

(1) Everyone charged with a penal offence has the right to be presumed innocent until proved guilty according to law in a public trial at which he has had all the guarantees necessary for his defence.

(2) No one shall be held guilty of any penal offence on account of any act or omission which did not constitute a penal offence, under national or international law, at the time when it was committed. Nor shall a heavier penalty be imposed than the one that was applicable at the time the penal offence was committed.

Article 12

No one shall be subjected to arbitrary interference with his privacy, family, home or correspondence, nor to attacks upon his honour and reputation. Everyone has the right to the protection of the law against such interference or attacks.

Article 13

(1) Everyone has the right to freedom of movement and residence within the borders of each state.

(2) Everyone has the right to leave any country, including his own, and to return to his country.

Article 14

(1) Everyone has the right to seek and to enjoy in other countries asylum from persecution.

(2) This right may not be invoked in the case of prosecutions genuinely arising from non-political crimes or from acts contrary to the purposes and principles of the United Nations.

Article 15

(1) Everyone has the right to a nationality.

(2) No one shall be arbitrarily deprived of his nationality nor denied the right to change his nationality.

Article 16

(1) Men and women of full age, without any limitation due to race, nationality or religion, have the right to marry and to found a family. They are entitled to equal rights as to marriage, during marriage and at its dissolution.

(2) Marriage shall be entered into only with the free and full consent of the intending spouses.

(3) The family is the natural and fundamental group unit of society and is entitled to protection by society and the State.

Article 17

(1) Everyone has the right to own property alone as well as in association with others.

(2) No one shall be arbitrarily deprived of his property.

Article 18

Everyone has the right to freedom of thought, conscience and religion; this right includes freedom to change his religion or belief, and freedom, either alone or in community with others and in public or private, to manifest his religion or belief in teaching, practice, worship and observance.

Article 19

Everyone has the right to freedom of opinion and expression; this right includes freedom to hold opinions without interference and to seek, receive and impart information and ideas through any media and regardless of frontiers.

Article 20

(1) Everyone has the right to freedom of peaceful assembly and association.

(2) No one may be compelled to belong to an association.

Article 21

(1) Everyone has the right to take part in the government of his country, directly or through freely chosen representatives.

(2) Everyone has the right to equal access to public service in his country.

(3) The will of the people shall be the basis of the authority of government; this shall be expressed in periodic and genuine elections which shall be by universal and equal suffrage and shall be held by secret vote or by equivalent free voting procedures.

Article 22

Everyone, as a member of society, has the right to social security and is entitled to realization, through national effort and international co-operation and in accordance with the organization and resources of each State, of the economic, social and cultural rights indispensable for his dignity and the free development of his personality.

Article 23

(1) Everyone has the right to work, to free choice of employment, to just and favourable conditions of work and to protection against unemployment.

(2) Everyone, without any discrimination, has the right to equal pay for equal work.

(3) Everyone who works has the right to just and favourable remuneration ensuring for himself and his family an existence worthy of human dignity, and supplemented, if necessary, by other means of social protection.

(4) Everyone has the right to form and to join trade unions for the protection of his interests.

Article 24

Everyone has the right to rest and leisure, including reasonable limitation of working hours and periodic holidays with pay.

Article 25

(1) Everyone has the right to a standard of living adequate for the health and well-being of himself and of his family, including food, clothing, housing and medical care and necessary social services, and the right to security in the event of unemployment, sickness, disability, widowhood, old age or other lack of livelihood in circumstances beyond his control.

(2) Motherhood and childhood are entitled to special care and assistance. All children, whether born in or out of wedlock, shall enjoy the same social protection.

Article 26

(1) Everyone has the right to education. Education shall be free, at least in the elementary and fundamental

stages. Elementary education shall be compulsory. Technical and professional education shall be made generally available and higher education shall be equally accessible to all on the basis of merit.

(2) Education shall be directed to the full development of the human personality and to the strengthening of respect for human rights and fundamental freedoms. It shall promote understanding, tolerance and friendship among all nations, racial or religious groups, and shall further the activities of the United Nations for the maintenance of peace.

(3) Parents have a prior right to choose the kind of education that shall be given to their children.

Article 27

(1) Everyone has the right freely to participate in the cultural life of the community, to enjoy the arts and to share in scientific advancement and its benefits.

(2) Everyone has the right to the protection of the moral and material interests resulting from any scientific, literary or artistic production of which he is the author.

Article 28

Everyone is entitled to a social and international order in which the rights and freedoms set forth in this Declaration can be fully realized.

Article 29

(1) Everyone has duties to the community in which alone the free and full development of his personality is possible.

(2) In the exercise of his rights and freedoms, everyone shall be subject only to such limitations as are determined by law solely for the purpose of securing

due recognition and respect for the rights and freedoms of others and of meeting the just requirements of morality, public order and the general welfare in a democratic society.

(3) These rights and freedoms may in no case be exercised contrary to the purposes and principles of the United Nations.

Article 30

Nothing in this Declaration may be interpreted as implying for any State, group or person any right to engage in any activity or to perform any act aimed at the destruction of any of the rights and freedoms set forth herein.

APPENDIX II

CONVENTION ON THE RIGHTS OF THE CHILD OF 1989

Adopted and opened for signature, ratification and accession by General Assembly resolution 44/25 of 20 November 1989 (entered into force 2 September 1990, in accordance with article 49)

PREAMBLE

The States Parties to the present Convention,

Considering that, in accordance with the principles proclaimed in the Charter of the United Nations, recognition of the inherent dignity and of the equal and inalienable rights of all members of the human family is the foundation of freedom, justice and peace in the world,

Bearing in mind that the peoples of the United Nations have, in the Charter, reaffirmed their faith in fundamental human rights and in the dignity and worth of the human person, and have determined to promote social progress and better standards of life in larger freedom,

Recognizing that the United Nations has, in the Universal Declaration of Human Rights and in the International Covenants on Human Rights, proclaimed and agreed that everyone is entitled to all the rights and freedoms set forth therein, without distinction of any kind, such as race, colour, sex, language, religion, political or other opinion, national or social origin, property, birth or other status,

Recalling that, in the Universal Declaration of Human Rights, the United Nations has proclaimed that childhood is entitled to special care and assistance,

Convinced that the family, as the fundamental group of

society and the natural environment for the growth and well-being of all its members and particularly children, should be afforded the necessary protection and assistance so that it can fully assume its responsibilities within the community,

Recognizing that the child, for the full and harmonious development of his or her personality, should grow up in a family environment, in an atmosphere of happiness, love and understanding,

Considering that the child should be fully prepared to live an individual life in society, and brought up in the spirit of the ideals proclaimed in the Charter of the United Nations, and in particular in the spirit of peace, dignity, tolerance, freedom, equality and solidarity,

Bearing in mind that the need to extend particular care to the child has been stated in the Geneva Declaration of the Rights of the Child of 1924 and in the Declaration of the Rights of the Child adopted by the General Assembly on 20 November 1959 and recognized in the Universal Declaration of Human Rights, in the International Covenant on Civil and Political Rights (in particular in articles 23 and 24), in the International Covenant on Economic, Social and Cultural Rights (in particular in article 10) and in the statutes and relevant instruments of specialized agencies and international organizations concerned with the welfare of children,

Bearing in mind that, as indicated in the Declaration of the Rights of the Child, "the child, by reason of his physical and mental immaturity, needs special safeguards and care, including appropriate legal protection, before as well as after birth",

Recalling the provisions of the Declaration on Social and Legal Principles relating to the Protection and Welfare of Children, with Special Reference to Foster Placement and Adoption Nationally and Internationally; the United Nations Standard Minimum Rules for the Administration of Juvenile Justice (The Beijing Rules); and the Declaration on the Protection of Women and Children in Emergency and Armed Conflict,

Recognizing that, in all countries in the world, there are children living in exceptionally difficult conditions, and that such children need special consideration,

Taking due account of the importance of the traditions and cultural values of each people for the protection and harmonious development of the child,

Recognizing the importance of international co-operation for improving the living conditions of children in every country, in particular in the developing countries,

Have agreed as follows:

PART I

Article 1

For the purposes of the present Convention, a child means every human being below the age of eighteen years unless, under the law applicable to the child, majority is attained earlier.

Article 2

1. States Parties shall respect and ensure the rights set forth in the present Convention to each child within their jurisdiction without discrimination of any kind, irrespective of the child's or his or her parent's or legal guardian's race, colour, sex, language, religion, political or other opinion, national, ethnic or social origin, property, disability, birth or other status.
2. States Parties shall take all appropriate measures to ensure that the child is protected against all forms of discrimination or punishment on the basis of the status, activities, expressed opinions, or beliefs of the child's parents, legal guardians, or family members.

Article 3

1. In all actions concerning children, whether undertaken by public or private social welfare institutions, courts of law, administrative authorities or legislative bodies, the best interests of the child shall be a primary consideration.
2. States Parties undertake to ensure the child such protection and care as is necessary for his or her well-being, taking into account the rights and duties of his or her parents, legal guardians, or other individuals legally responsible for him or her, and, to this end, shall take all appropriate legislative and administrative measures.
3. States Parties shall ensure that the institutions, services and facilities responsible for the care or protection of children shall conform with the standards established by competent authorities, particularly in the areas of safety, health, in the number and suitability of their staff, as well as competent supervision.

Article 4

States Parties shall undertake all appropriate legislative, administrative, and other measures for the implementation of the rights recognized in the present Convention. With regard to economic, social and cultural rights, States Parties shall undertake such measures to the maximum extent of their available resources and, where needed, within the framework of international co-operation.

Article 5

States Parties shall respect the responsibilities, rights and duties of parents or, where applicable, the members of the extended family or community as provided for by local custom, legal guardians or other persons legally responsible for the child, to provide, in a manner consistent with the evolving capacities of the child, appropriate direction and guidance in the exercise by the child of the rights recognized in the present Convention.

Article 6

1. States Parties recognize that every child has the inherent right to life.
2. States Parties shall ensure to the maximum extent possible the survival and development of the child.

Article 7

1. The child shall be registered immediately after birth and shall have the right from birth to a name, the right to acquire a nationality and, as far as possible, the right to know and be cared for by his or her parents.
2. States Parties shall ensure the implementation of these rights in accordance with their national law and their obligations under the relevant international instruments in this field, in particular where the child would otherwise be stateless.

Article 8

1. States Parties undertake to respect the right of the child to preserve his or her identity, including nationality, name and family relations as recognized by law without unlawful interference.
2. Where a child is illegally deprived of some or all of the elements of his or her identity, States Parties shall provide appropriate assistance and protection, with a view to re-establishing speedily his or her identity.

Article 9

1. States Parties shall ensure that a child shall not be

separated from his or her parents against their will, except when competent authorities subject to judicial review determine, in accordance with applicable law and procedures, that such separation is necessary for the best interests of the child. Such determination may be necessary in a particular case such as one involving abuse or neglect of the child by the parents, or one where the parents are living separately and a decision must be made as to the child's place of residence.

2. In any proceedings pursuant to paragraph 1 of the present article, all interested parties shall be given an opportunity to participate in the proceedings and make their views known.

3. States Parties shall respect the right of the child who is separated from one or both parents to maintain personal relations and direct contact with both parents on a regular basis, except if it is contrary to the child's best interests.

4. Where such separation results from any action initiated by a State Party, such as the detention, imprisonment, exile, deportation or death (including death arising from any cause while the person is in the custody of the State) of one or both parents or of the child, that State Party shall, upon request, provide the parents, the child or, if appropriate, another member of the family with the essential information concerning the whereabouts of the absent member(s) of the family unless the provision of the information would be detrimental to the well-being of the child. States Parties shall further ensure that the submission of such a request shall of itself entail no adverse consequences for the person(s) concerned.

Article 10

1. In accordance with the obligation of States Parties under article 9, paragraph 1, applications by a child or his or her parents to enter or leave a State Party for the

purpose of family reunification shall be dealt with by States Parties in a positive, humane and expeditious manner. States Parties shall further ensure that the submission of such a request shall entail no adverse consequences for the applicants and for the members of their family.

2. A child whose parents reside in different States shall have the right to maintain on a regular basis, save in exceptional circumstances, personal relations and direct contacts with both parents. Towards that end and in accordance with the obligation of States Parties under article 9, paragraph 1, States Parties shall respect the right of the child and his or her parents to leave any country, including their own, and to enter their own country. The right to leave any country shall be subject only to such restrictions as are prescribed by law and which are necessary to protect the national security, public order (*ordre public*), public health or morals or the rights and freedoms of others and are consistent with the other rights recognized in the present Convention.

Article 11

1. States Parties shall take measures to combat the illicit transfer and non-return of children abroad.
2. To this end, States Parties shall promote the conclusion of bilateral or multilateral agreements or accession to existing agreements.

Article 12

1. States Parties shall assure to the child who is capable of forming his or her own views the right to express those views freely in all matters affecting the child, the views of the child being given due weight in accordance with the age and maturity of the child.
2. For this purpose, the child shall in particular be provided

the opportunity to be heard in any judicial and administrative proceedings affecting the child, either directly, or through a representative or an appropriate body, in a manner consistent with the procedural rules of national law.

Article 13

1. The child shall have the right to freedom of expression; this right shall include freedom to seek, receive and impart information and ideas of all kinds, regardless of frontiers, either orally, in writing or in print, in the form of art, or through any other media of the child's choice.
2. The exercise of this right may be subject to certain restrictions, but these shall only be such as are provided by law and are necessary:
   (a) For respect of the rights or reputations of others; or
   (b) For the protection of national security or of public order (*ordre public*), or of public health or morals.

Article 14

1. States Parties shall respect the right of the child to freedom of thought, conscience and religion.
2. States Parties shall respect the rights and duties of the parents and, when applicable, legal guardians, to provide direction to the child in the exercise of his or her right in a manner consistent with the evolving capacities of the child.
3. Freedom to manifest one's religion or beliefs may be subject only to such limitations as are prescribed by law and are necessary to protect public safety, order, health or morals, or the fundamental rights and freedoms of others.

Article 15

1. States Parties recognize the rights of the child to freedom of association and to freedom of peaceful assembly.
2. No restrictions may be placed on the exercise of these rights other than those imposed in conformity with the law and which are necessary in a democratic society in the interests of national security or public safety, public order (*ordre public*), the protection of public health or morals or the protection of the rights and freedoms of others.

Article 16

1. No child shall be subjected to arbitrary or unlawful interference with his or her privacy, family, home or correspondence, nor to unlawful attacks on his or her honour and reputation.
2. The child has the right to the protection of the law against such interference or attacks.

Article 17

States Parties recognize the important function performed by the mass media and shall ensure that the child has access to information and material from a diversity of national and international sources, especially those aimed at the promotion of his or her social, spiritual and moral well-being and physical and mental health. To this end, States Parties shall:

(a) Encourage the mass media to disseminate information and material of social and cultural benefit to the child and in accordance with the spirit of article 29;

(b) Encourage international co-operation in the production, exchange and dissemination of such information and material from a diversity of cultural, national and international sources;

(c) Encourage the production and dissemination of children's books;

(d)Encourage the mass media to have particular regard to the linguistic needs of the child who belongs to a minority group or who is indigenous;

(e)Encourage the development of appropriate guidelines for the protection of the child from information and material injurious to his or her well-being, bearing in mind the provisions of articles 13 and 18.

Article 18

1. States Parties shall use their best efforts to ensure recognition of the principle that both parents have common responsibilities for the upbringing and development of the child. Parents or, as the case may be, legal guardians, have the primary responsibility for the upbringing and development of the child. The best interests of the child will be their basic concern.
2. For the purpose of guaranteeing and promoting the rights set forth in the present Convention, States Parties shall render appropriate assistance to parents and legal guardians in the performance of their child-rearing responsibilities and shall ensure the development of institutions, facilities and services for the care of children.
3. States Parties shall take all appropriate measures to ensure that children of working parents have the right to benefit from child-care services and facilities for which they are eligible.

Article 19

1. States Parties shall take all appropriate legislative, administrative, social and educational measures to protect the child from all forms of physical or mental violence, injury or abuse, neglect or negligent treatment, maltreatment or exploitation, including sexual abuse,

while in the care of parent(s), legal guardian(s) or any other person who has the care of the child.

2. Such protective measures should, as appropriate, include effective procedures for the establishment of social programmes to provide necessary support for the child and for those who have the care of the child, as well as for other forms of prevention and for identification, reporting, referral, investigation, treatment and follow-up of instances of child maltreatment described heretofore, and, as appropriate, for judicial involvement.

Article 20

1. A child temporarily or permanently deprived of his or her family environment, or in whose own best interests cannot be allowed to remain in that environment, shall be entitled to special protection and assistance provided by the State.
2. States Parties shall in accordance with their national laws ensure alternative care for such a child.
3. Such care could include, *inter alia*, foster placement, *kafalah* of Islamic law, adoption or if necessary placement in suitable institutions for the care of children. When considering solutions, due regard shall be paid to the desirability of continuity in a child's upbringing and to the child's ethnic, religious, cultural and linguistic background.

Article 21

States Parties that recognize and/or permit the system of adoption shall ensure that the best interests of the child shall be the paramount consideration and they shall:

(a) Ensure that the adoption of a child is authorized only by competent authorities who determine, in accordance with applicable law and procedures and on the basis of all pertinent and reliable information, that the adoption is permissible in view of the child's status concerning parents, relatives and legal guardians and that, if required, the persons concerned have given their informed consent to the adoption on the basis of such counselling as may be necessary;

(b) Recognize that inter-country adoption may be considered as an alternative means of child's care, if the child cannot be placed in a foster or an adoptive family or cannot in any suitable manner be cared for in the child's country of origin;

(c) Ensure that the child concerned by inter-country adoption enjoys safeguards and standards equivalent to those existing in the case of national adoption;

(d) Take all appropriate measures to ensure that, in inter-country adoption, the placement does not result in improper financial gain for those involved in it;

(e) Promote, where appropriate, the objectives of the present article by concluding bilateral or multilateral arrangements or agreements, and endeavour, within this framework, to ensure that the placement of the child in another country is carried out by competent authorities or organs.

Article 22

1. States Parties shall take appropriate measures to ensure that a child who is seeking refugee status or who is considered a refugee in accordance with applicable international or domestic law and procedures shall, whether unaccompanied or accompanied by his or her parents or by any other person, receive appropriate protection and humanitarian assistance in the enjoyment of applicable rights set forth in the present Convention and in other international human rights or humanitarian instruments to which the said States are Parties.

2. For this purpose, States Parties shall provide, as they consider appropriate, co-operation in any efforts by the United Nations and other competent intergovernmental organizations or non-governmental organizations co-

operating with the United Nations to protect and assist such a child and to trace the parents or other members of the family of any refugee child in order to obtain information necessary for reunification with his or her family. In cases where no parents or other members of the family can be found, the child shall be accorded the same protection as any other child permanently or temporarily deprived of his or her family environment for any reason, as set forth in the present Convention.

Article 23

1. States Parties recognize that a mentally or physically disabled child should enjoy a full and decent life, in conditions which ensure dignity, promote self-reliance and facilitate the child's active participation in the community.
2. States Parties recognize the right of the disabled child to special care and shall encourage and ensure the extension, subject to available resources, to the eligible child and those responsible for his or her care, of assistance for which application is made and which is appropriate to the child's condition and to the circumstances of the parents or others caring for the child.
3. Recognizing the special needs of a disabled child, assistance extended in accordance with paragraph 2 of the present article shall be provided free of charge, whenever possible, taking into account the financial resources of the parents or others caring for the child, and shall be designed to ensure that the disabled child has effective access to and receives education, training, health care services, rehabilitation services, preparation for employment and recreation opportunities in a manner conducive to the child's achieving the fullest possible social integration and individual development, including his or her cultural and spiritual development
4. States Parties shall promote, in the spirit of international

co-operation, the exchange of appropriate information in the field of preventive health care and of medical, psychological and functional treatment of disabled children, including dissemination of and access to information concerning methods of rehabilitation, education and vocational services, with the aim of enabling States Parties to improve their capabilities and skills and to widen their experience in these areas. In this regard, particular account shall be taken of the needs of developing countries.

Article 24

1. States Parties recognize the right of the child to the enjoyment of the highest attainable standard of health and to facilities for the treatment of illness and rehabilitation of health. States Parties shall strive to ensure that no child is deprived of his or her right of access to such health care services.
2. States Parties shall pursue full implementation of this right and, in particular, shall take appropriate measures:
   (a) To diminish infant and child mortality;
   (b) To ensure the provision of necessary medical assistance and health care to all children with emphasis on the development of primary health care;
   (c) To combat disease and malnutrition, including within the framework of primary health care, through, *inter alia*, the application of readily available technology and through the provision of adequate nutritious foods and clean drinking-water, taking into consideration the dangers and risks of environmental pollution;
   (d) To ensure appropriate pre-natal and post-natal health care for mothers;
   (e) To ensure that all segments of society, in particular parents and children, are informed, have access to

education and are supported in the use of basic knowledge of child health and nutrition, the advantages of breastfeeding, hygiene and environmental sanitation and the prevention of accidents;

(f) To develop preventive health care, guidance for parents and family planning education and services.

3. States Parties shall take all effective and appropriate measures with a view to abolishing traditional practices prejudicial to the health of children.
4. States Parties undertake to promote and encourage international co-operation with a view to achieving progressively the full realization of the right recognized in the present article. In this regard, particular account shall be taken of the needs of developing countries.

Article 25

States Parties recognize the right of a child who has been placed by the competent authorities for the purposes of care, protection or treatment of his or her physical or mental health, to a periodic review of the treatment provided to the child and all other circumstances relevant to his or her placement.

Article 26

1. States Parties shall recognize for every child the right to benefit from social security, including social insurance, and shall take the necessary measures to achieve the full realization of this right in accordance with their national law.
2. The benefits should, where appropriate, be granted, taking into account the resources and the circumstances of the child and persons having responsibility for the maintenance of the child, as well as any other consideration relevant to an application for benefits made by or on behalf of the child.

Article 27

1. States Parties recognize the right of every child to a standard of living adequate for the child's physical, mental, spiritual, moral and social development.
2. The parent(s) or others responsible for the child have the primary responsibility to secure, within their abilities and financial capacities, the conditions of living necessary for the child's development.
3. States Parties, in accordance with national conditions and within their means, shall take appropriate measures to assist parents and others responsible for the child to implement this right and shall in case of need provide material assistance and support programmes, particularly with regard to nutrition, clothing and housing.
4. States Parties shall take all appropriate measures to secure the recovery of maintenance for the child from the parents or other persons having financial responsibility for the child, both within the State Party and from abroad. In particular, where the person having financial responsibility for the child lives in a State different from that of the child, States Parties shall promote the accession to international agreements or the conclusion of such agreements, as well as the making of other appropriate arrangements.

Article 28

1. States Parties recognize the right of the child to education, and with a view to achieving this right progressively and on the basis of equal opportunity, they shall, in particular:

(a) Make primary education compulsory and available free to all;

(b) Encourage the development of different forms of secondary education, including general and vocational education, make them available and accessible to every child, and take appropriate measures such as the introduction of free education and offering financial assistance in case of need;

(c) Make higher education accessible to all on the basis of capacity by every appropriate means;

(d) Make educational and vocational information and guidance available and accessible to all children;

(e) Take measures to encourage regular attendance at schools and the reduction of drop-out rates.

2. States Parties shall take all appropriate measures to ensure that school discipline is administered in a manner consistent with the child's human dignity and in conformity with the present Convention.

3. States Parties shall promote and encourage international co-operation in matters relating to education, in particular with a view to contributing to the elimination of ignorance and illiteracy throughout the world and facilitating access to scientific and technical knowledge and modern teaching methods. In this regard, particular account shall be taken of the needs of developing countries.

Article 29

1. States Parties agree that the education of the child shall be directed to:

(a) The development of the child's personality, talents and mental and physical abilities to their fullest potential;

(b) The development of respect for human rights and fundamental freedoms, and for the principles enshrined in the Charter of the United Nations;

(c) The development of respect for the child's parents, his or her own cultural identity, language and values, for the national values of the country in which the child is living, the country from which he or she may originate, and for civilizations different from his or her own;

(d) The preparation of the child for responsible life in a free society, in the spirit of understanding, peace, tolerance, equality of sexes, and friendship among all peoples, ethnic, national and religious groups and persons of indigenous origin;

(e) The development of respect for the natural environment.

2. No part of the present article or article 28 shall be construed so as to interfere with the liberty of individuals and bodies to establish and direct educational institutions, subject always to the observance of the principle set forth in paragraph 1 of the present article and to the requirements that the education given in such institutions shall conform to such minimum standards as may be laid down by the State.

Article 30

In those States in which ethnic, religious or linguistic minorities or persons of indigenous origin exist, a child belonging to such a minority or who is indigenous shall not be denied the right, in community with other members of his or her group, to enjoy his or her own culture, to profess and practise his or her own religion, or to use his or her own language.

Article 31

1. States Parties recognize the right of the child to rest and leisure, to engage in play and recreational activities appropriate to the age of the child and to participate freely in cultural life and the arts.

2. States Parties shall respect and promote the right of the child to participate fully in cultural and artistic life and shall encourage the provision of appropriate and equal opportunities for cultural, artistic, recreational and leisure activity.

Article 32

1. States Parties recognize the right of the child to be protected from economic exploitation and from performing any work that is likely to be hazardous or to interfere with the child's education, or to be harmful to the child's health or physical, mental, spiritual, moral or social development.
2. States Parties shall take legislative, administrative, social and educational measures to ensure the implementation of the present article. To this end, and having regard to the relevant provisions of other international instruments, States Parties shall in particular:
   (a) Provide for a minimum age or minimum ages for admission to employment;
   (b) Provide for appropriate regulation of the hours and conditions of employment;
   (c) Provide for appropriate penalties or other sanctions to ensure the effective enforcement of the present article.

Article 33

States Parties shall take all appropriate measures, including legislative, administrative, social and educational measures, to protect children from the illicit use of narcotic drugs and psychotropic substances as defined in the relevant international treaties, and to prevent the use of children in the illicit production and trafficking of such substances.

Article 34

States Parties undertake to protect the child from all forms of sexual exploitation and sexual abuse. For these purposes, States Parties shall in particular take all appropriate national, bilateral and multilateral measures to prevent:

(a) The inducement or coercion of a child to engage in any unlawful sexual activity;

(b) The exploitative use of children in prostitution or other unlawful sexual practices;

(c) The exploitative use of children in pornographic performances and materials.

Article 35

States Parties shall take all appropriate national, bilateral and multilateral measures to prevent the abduction of, the sale of or traffic in children for any purpose or in any form.

Article 36

States Parties shall protect the child against all other forms of exploitation prejudicial to any aspects of the child's welfare.

Article 37

States Parties shall ensure that:

(a) No child shall be subjected to torture or other cruel, inhuman or degrading treatment or punishment. Neither capital punishment nor life imprisonment without possibility of release shall be imposed for offences committed by persons below eighteen years of age;

(b) No child shall be deprived of his or her liberty unlawfully or arbitrarily. The arrest, detention or imprisonment of a child shall be in conformity with the law and shall be used only as a measure of last resort and for the shortest appropriate period of time;

(c) Every child deprived of liberty shall be treated with humanity and respect for the inherent dignity of the human person, and in a manner which takes into account the needs of persons of his or her age. In particular, every child deprived of liberty shall be separated from adults unless it is considered in the child's best interest not to do so and shall have the right to maintain contact with his or her family through correspondence and visits, save in exceptional circumstances;

(d) Every child deprived of his or her liberty shall have the right to prompt access to legal and other appropriate assistance, as well as the right to challenge the legality of the deprivation of his or her liberty before a court or other competent, independent and impartial authority, and to a prompt decision on any such action.

Article 38

1. States Parties undertake to respect and to ensure respect for rules of international humanitarian law applicable to them in armed conflicts which are relevant to the child.
2. States Parties shall take all feasible measures to ensure that persons who have not attained the age of fifteen years do not take a direct part in hostilities.
3. States Parties shall refrain from recruiting any person who has not attained the age of fifteen years into their armed forces. In recruiting among those persons who have attained the age of fifteen years but who have not attained the age of eighteen years, States Parties shall endeavour to give priority to those who are oldest.
4. In accordance with their obligations under international humanitarian law to protect the civilian population in armed conflicts, States Parties shall take all feasible measures to ensure protection and care of children who are affected by an armed conflict.

Article 39

States Parties shall take all appropriate measures to promote physical and psychological recovery and social reintegration of a child victim of: any form of neglect, exploitation, or abuse; torture or any other form of cruel, inhuman or degrading treatment or punishment; or armed conflicts. Such recovery and reintegration shall take place in an environment which fosters the health, self-respect and dignity of the child.

Article 40

1. States Parties recognize the right of every child alleged as, accused of, or recognized as having infringed the penal law to be treated in a manner consistent with the promotion of the child's sense of dignity and worth, which reinforces the child's respect for the human rights and fundamental freedoms of others and which takes into account the child's age and the desirability of promoting the child's reintegration and the child's assuming a constructive role in society.
2. To this end, and having regard to the relevant provisions of international instruments, States Parties shall, in particular, ensure that:
   (a) No child shall be alleged as, be accused of, or recognized as having infringed the penal law by reason of acts or omissions that were not prohibited by national or international law at the time they were committed;
   (b) Every child alleged as or accused of having infringed the penal law has at least the following guarantees:
      (i) To be presumed innocent until proven guilty according to law;
      (ii) To be informed promptly and directly of the charges against him or her, and, if appropriate, through his or her parents or legal guardians, and to have legal or other appropriate assistance in the preparation and presentation of his or her defence;
      (iii) To have the matter determined without delay by a competent, independent and impartial authority or judicial body in a fair hearing according to law, in the presence of legal or

other appropriate assistance and, unless it is considered not to be in the best interest of the child, in particular, taking into account his or her age or situation, his or her parents or legal guardians;

(iv) Not to be compelled to give testimony or to confess guilt; to examine or have examined adverse witnesses and to obtain the participation and examination of witnesses on his or her behalf under conditions of equality;

(v) If considered to have infringed the penal law, to have this decision and any measures imposed in consequence thereof reviewed by a higher competent, independent and impartial authority or judicial body according to law;

(vi) To have the free assistance of an interpreter if the child cannot understand or speak the language used;

(vii) To have his or her privacy fully respected at all stages of the proceedings.

3. States Parties shall seek to promote the establishment of laws, procedures, authorities and institutions specifically applicable to children alleged as, accused of, or recognized as having infringed the penal law, and, in particular:

(a) The establishment of a minimum age below which children shall be presumed not to have the capacity to infringe the penal law;

(b) Whenever appropriate and desirable, measures for dealing with such children without resorting to judicial proceedings, providing that human rights and legal safeguards are fully respected.

4. A variety of dispositions, such as care, guidance and supervision orders; counselling; probation; foster care; education and vocational training programmes and other alternatives to institutional care shall be available to ensure that children are dealt with in a manner

appropriate to their well-being and proportionate both to their circumstances and the offence.

Article 41

Nothing in the present Convention shall affect any provisions which are more conducive to the realization of the rights of the child and which may be contained in:

(a) The law of a State party; or

(b) International law in force for that State.

PART II

Article 42

States Parties undertake to make the principles and provisions of the Convention widely known, by appropriate and active means, to adults and children alike.

Article 43

1. For the purpose of examining the progress made by States Parties in achieving the realization of the obligations undertaken in the present Convention, there shall be established a Committee on the Rights of the Child, which shall carry out the functions hereinafter provided.
2. The Committee shall consist of ten experts of high moral standing and recognized competence in the field covered by this Convention. The members of the Committee shall be elected by States Parties from among their nationals and shall serve in their personal capacity, consideration being given to equitable geographical distribution, as well as to the principal legal systems.
3. The members of the Committee shall be elected by secret ballot from a list of persons nominated by States Parties. Each State Party may nominate one person from among its own nationals.

4. The initial election to the Committee shall be held no later than six months after the date of the entry into force of the present Convention and thereafter every second year. At least four months before the date of each election, the Secretary-General of the United Nations shall address a letter to States Parties inviting them to submit their nominations within two months. The Secretary-General shall subsequently prepare a list in alphabetical order of all persons thus nominated, indicating States Parties which have nominated them, and shall submit it to the States Parties to the present Convention.
5. The elections shall be held at meetings of States Parties convened by the Secretary-General at United Nations Headquarters. At those meetings, for which two thirds of States Parties shall constitute a quorum, the persons elected to the Committee shall be those who obtain the largest number of votes and an absolute majority of the votes of the representatives of States Parties present and voting.
6. The members of the Committee shall be elected for a term of four years. They shall be eligible for re-election if renominated. The term of five of the members elected at the first election shall expire at the end of two years; immediately after the first election, the names of these five members shall be chosen by lot by the Chairman of the meeting.
7. If a member of the Committee dies or resigns or declares that for any other cause he or she can no longer perform the duties of the Committee, the State Party which nominated the member shall appoint another expert from among its nationals to serve for the remainder of the term, subject to the approval of the Committee.
8. The Committee shall establish its own rules of procedure.
9. The Committee shall elect its officers for a period of two years.

10. The meetings of the Committee shall normally be held at United Nations Headquarters or at any other convenient place as determined by the Committee. The Committee shall normally meet annually. The duration of the meetings of the Committee shall be determined, and reviewed, if necessary, by a meeting of the States Parties to the present Convention, subject to the approval of the General Assembly.
11. The Secretary-General of the United Nations shall provide the necessary staff and facilities for the effective performance of the functions of the Committee under the present Convention.
12. With the approval of the General Assembly, the members of the Committee established under the present Convention shall receive emoluments from United Nations resources on such terms and conditions as the Assembly may decide.

Article 44

1. States Parties undertake to submit to the Committee, through the Secretary-General of the United Nations, reports on the measures they have adopted which give effect to the rights recognized herein and on the progress made on the enjoyment of those rights:
   (a) Within two years of the entry into force of the Convention for the State Party concerned;
   (b) Thereafter every five years.
2. Reports made under the present article shall indicate factors and difficulties, if any, affecting the degree of fulfilment of the obligations under the present Convention. Reports shall also contain sufficient information to provide the Committee with a comprehensive understanding of the implementation of the Convention in the country concerned.
3. A State Party which has submitted a comprehensive initial report to the Committee need not, in its

subsequent reports submitted in accordance with paragraph 1(b) of the present article, repeat basic information previously provided.

4. The Committee may request from States Parties further information relevant to the implementation of the Convention.
5. The Committee shall submit to the General Assembly, through the Economic and Social Council, every two years, reports on its activities.
6. States Parties shall make their reports widely available to the public in their own countries.

Article 45

In order to foster the effective implementation of the Convention and to encourage international co-operation in the field covered by the Convention:

(a) The specialized agencies, the United Nations Children's Fund, and other United Nations organs shall be entitled to be represented at the consideration of the implementation of such provisions of the present Convention as fall within the scope of their mandate. The Committee may invite the specialized agencies, the United Nations Children's Fund and other competent bodies as it may consider appropriate to provide expert advice on the implementation of the Convention in areas falling within the scope of their respective mandates. The Committee may invite the specialized agencies, the United Nations Children's Fund, and other United Nations organs to submit reports on the implementation of the Convention in areas falling within the scope of their activities;

(b) The Committee shall transmit, as it may consider appropriate, to the specialized agencies, the United Nations Children's Fund and other competent bodies, any reports from States Parties that contain a request, or indicate a need, for technical advice or assistance, along with the Committee's observations and suggestions, if any, on these requests or indications;

(c) The Committee may recommend to the General Assembly to request the Secretary-General to undertake on its behalf studies on specific issues relating to the rights of the child;

(d) The Committee may make suggestions and general recommendations based on information received pursuant to articles 44 and 45 of the present Convention. Such suggestions and general recommendations shall be transmitted to any State Party concerned and reported to the General Assembly, together with comments, if any, from States Parties.

PART III

Article 46

The present Convention shall be open for signature by all States.

Article 47

The present Convention is subject to ratification. Instruments of ratification shall be deposited with the Secretary-General of the United Nations.

Article 48

The present Convention shall remain open for accession by any State. The instruments of accession shall be deposited with the Secretary-General of the United Nations.

Article 49

1. The present Convention shall enter into force on the thirtieth day following the date of deposit with the Secretary-General of the United Nations of the twentieth instrument of ratification or accession.

2. For each State ratifying or acceding to the Convention after the deposit of the twentieth instrument of ratification or accession, the Convention shall enter into force on the thirtieth day after the deposit by such State of its instrument of ratification or accession.

Article 50

1. Any State Party may propose an amendment and file it with the Secretary-General of the United Nations. The Secretary-General shall thereupon communicate the proposed amendment to States Parties, with a request that they indicate whether they favour a conference of States Parties for the purpose of considering and voting upon the proposals. In the event that, within four months from the date of such communication, at least one third of the States Parties favour such a conference, the Secretary-General shall convene the conference under the auspices of the United Nations. Any amendment adopted by a majority of States Parties present and voting at the conference shall be submitted to the General Assembly for approval.
2. An amendment adopted in accordance with paragraph 1 of the present article shall enter into force when it has been approved by the General Assembly of the United Nations and accepted by a two-thirds majority of States Parties.
3. When an amendment enters into force, it shall be binding on those States Parties which have accepted it, other States Parties still being bound by the provisions of the present Convention and any earlier amendments which they have accepted.

Article 51

1. The Secretary-General of the United Nations shall receive and circulate to all States the text of reservations made by States at the time of ratification or accession.

2. A reservation incompatible with the object and purpose of the present Convention shall not be permitted.
3. Reservations may be withdrawn at any time by notification to that effect addressed to the Secretary-General of the United Nations, who shall then inform all States. Such notification shall take effect on the date on which it is received by the Secretary-General

Article 52

A State Party may denounce the present Convention by written notification to the Secretary-General of the United Nations. Denunciation becomes effective one year after the date of receipt of the notification by the Secretary-General.

Article 53

The Secretary-General of the United Nations is designated as the depositary of the present Convention.

Article 54

The original of the present Convention, of which the Arabic, Chinese, English, French, Russian and Spanish texts are equally authentic, shall be deposited with the Secretary-General of the United Nations.

IN WITNESS THEREOF the undersigned plenipotentiaries, being duly authorized thereto by their respective Governments, have signed the present Convention.

APPENDIX III

THE PROTECTION OF HUMAN RIGHTS ACT, 1993

(entered into force 28 September 1993)

An Act to provide for the constitution of a National Human Rights Commission, State Human Rights Commission in States and Human Rights Courts for better protection of human rights and for matters connected therewith or incidental thereto.

Be it enacted by the Parliament in the Forty-fourth year of the Republic of India as follows:-

Chapter I

PRELIMINARY

1. Short title, extent and commencement

(1) This Act may be called the Protection of Human Rights Act, 1993.

(2) It extends to the whole of India:

Provided that it shall apply to the State of Jammu and Kashmir only in so far as it pertains to the matters relatable to any of the entries enumerated in List I or List III in the Seventh Schedule to the Constitution as applicable to that State.

(3) It shall be deemed to have come into force on the 28th day of September 1993.

2. Definitions

(1) In this Act, unless the context otherwise requires.—

(a) "armed forces" means the naval, military and air forces and includes any other armed forces of the Union;

(b) "Chairperson" means the Chairperson of the Commission or of the State Commission, as the case may be;

(c) "Commission" means the National Human Rights Commission constituted under section 3;

(d) "human rights" means the rights relating to life, liberty, equality and dignity of the individual guaranteed by the Constitution or embodied in the International Covenants and enforceable by courts in India.

(e) "Human Rights Court" means the Human Rights Court specified under section 30;

(f) "International Covenants" means the International Covenant on Civil and Political Rights and the International Covenant on Economic, Social and Cultural Rights adopted by the General Assembly of the United Nations on the 16th December, 1966;

(g) "Member" means a Member of the Commission or of the State Commission, as the case may be, and includes the Chairperson;

(h) "National Commission for Minorities" means the National Commission for Minorities constituted under section 3 of the National Commission for Minorities Act, 1992;

(i) "National Commission for the Scheduled Castes and Scheduled Tribes" means the National Commission for the Scheduled Castes and Scheduled Tribes referred to in Article 338 of the Constitution;

(j) "National Commission for Women" means the National Commission for Women constituted under section 3 of the National Commission for Women Act, 1990;

(k) "notification" means a notification published in the Official Gazette;

(l) "prescribed" means prescribed by rules made under this Act;

(m) "public servant" shall have the meaning assigned to it in section 21 of the Indian Penal Code;

(n) "State Commission" means a State Human Rights Commission constituted under section 21.

(2) Any reference in this Act to a law, which is not in force in the State of Jammu and Kashmir, shall, in relation to that State, be construed as a reference to a corresponding law, if any, in force in that State.

Chapter II

THE NATIONAL HUMAN RIGHTS COMMISSION

3. Constitution of a National Human Rights Commission

(1) The Central Government shall constitute a body to be known as the National Human Rights Commission to exercise the powers conferred upon, and to perform the functions assigned to it, under this Act.

(2) The Commission shall consist of —

(a) a Chairperson who has been a Chief Justice of the Supreme Court;

(b) one Member who is, or has been, a Judge of the Supreme Court;

(c) one Member who is, or has been, the Chief Justice of a High Court;

(d) two Members to be appointed from amongst persons having knowledge of, or practical experience in, matters relating to human rights.

(3) The Chairpersons of the National Commission for Minorities, the National Commission for the Scheduled Castes and Scheduled Tribes and the National Commission for Women shall be deemed to be Members of the Commission for the discharge of functions specified in clauses (b) to (j) of section 12.

(4) There shall be a Secretary-General who shall be the Chief Executive Officer of the Commission and shall exercise such powers and discharge such functions of the Commission as it may delegate to him.

(5) The headquarters of the Commission shall be at Delhi and the Commission may, with the previous approval of the Central Government, establish offices at other places in India.

4. Appointment of Chairperson and other Members

(1) The Chairperson and other Members shall be appointed by the President by warrant under his hand and seal:

Provided that every appointment under this sub-section shall be made after obtaining the recommendations of a Committee consisting of —

(a) the Prime Minister —Chairperson;

(b) Speaker of the House of the People —Member;

(c) Minister in-charge of the Ministry of Home Affairs in the Government of India —Member;

(d) Leader of the Opposition in the House of the People —Member;

(e) Leader of the Opposition in the Council of States —Member;

(f) Deputy Chairman of the Council of States—Member:

Provided further that no sitting Judge of the Supreme Court or sitting Chief Justice of a High Court shall be appointed except after consultation with the Chief Justice of India.

(2) No appointment of a Chairperson or a Member shall be invalid merely by reason of any vacancy in the Committee.

5. Removal of a Member of the Commission

(1) Subject to the provisions of sub-section (2), the Chairperson or any other Member of the Commission shall only be removed from his office by order of the President on the ground of proved misbehaviour or incapacity after the Supreme Court, on reference being made to it by the President, has, on inquiry held in accordance with the procedure prescribed in that behalf by the Supreme Court, reported that the Chairperson

or such other Member, as the case may be, ought on any such ground to be removed.

(2) Notwithstanding anything in sub-section (1), the President may by order remove from office the Chairperson or any other Member if the Chairperson or such other Member, as the case may be, —

(a) is adjudged an insolvent; or

(b) engages during his term of office in any paid employment out side the duties of his office; or

(c) is unfit to continue in office by reason of infirmity of mind or body; or

(d) is of unsound mind and stands so declared by a competent court; or

(e) is convicted and sentenced to imprisonment for an offence which in the opinion of the President involves moral turpitude.

6. Term of Office of Members

(1) A person appointed as Chairperson shall hold office for a term of five years from the date on which he enters upon his office or until he attains the age of seventy years, whichever is earlier.

(2) A person appointed as a Member shall hold office for a term of five years from the date on which he enters upon his office and shall be eligible for re-appointment for another term of five years:

Provided that no Member shall hold office after he has attained the age of seventy years.

(3) On ceasing to hold office, a Chairperson or a Member shall be ineligible for further employment under the Government of India or under the Government of any State.

7. Member to Act as Chairperson or to Discharge His Functions in Certain Circumstances

(1) In the event of the occurrence of any vacancy in the office of the Chairperson by reason of his death, resignation or otherwise, the President may, by

notification, authorise one of the Members to act as the Chairperson until the appointment of a new Chairperson to fill such vacancy.

(2) When the Chairperson is unable to discharge his functions owing to absence on leave or otherwise, such one of the Members as the President may, by notification, authorise in this behalf, shall discharge the functions of the Chairperson until the date on which the Chairperson resumes his duties.

8. Terms and conditions of service of Members

The salaries and allowances payable to, and other terms and conditions of service of, the Members shall be such as may be prescribed:

Provided that neither the salary and allowances nor the other terms and conditions of service of a Member shall be varied to his disadvantage after his appointment.

9. Vacancies, etc., not to invalidate the proceedings of the Commission

No act or proceedings of the Commission shall be questioned or shall be invalidated merely on the ground of existence of any vacancy or defect in the constitution of the Commission.

10. Procedure to be regulated by the Commission

(1) The Commission shall meet at such time and place as the Chairperson may think fit.

(2) The Commission shall regulate its own procedure.

(3) All orders and decisions of the Commission shall be authenticated by the Secretary-General or any other officer of the Commission duly authorised by the Chairperson in this behalf.

11. Officers and other staff of the Commission

(1) The Central Government shall make available to the Commission—

(a) an officer of the rank of the Secretary to the Government of India who shall be the Secretary-General of the Commission; and

(b) such police and investigative staff under an officer not below the rank of a Director General of Police and such other officers and staff as may be necessary for the efficient performance of the functions of the Commission.

(2) Subject to such rules as may be made by the Central Government in this behalf, the Commission may appoint such other administrative, technical and scientific staff as it may consider necessary.

(3) The salaries, allowances and conditions of service of the officers and other staff appointed under sub-section (2) shall be such as may be prescribed.

Chapter III

FUNCLTIONS AND POWERS OF THE COMMISSION

12. Functions of the Commission

The Commission shall perform all or any of the following functions, namely:—

(a) inquire, *suo motu* or on a petition presented to it by a victim or any person on his behalf, into complaint of—

(i) violation of human rights or abetment thereof; or

(ii) negligence in the prevention of such violation, by a public servant;

(b) intervene in any proceeding involving any allegation of violation of human rights pending before a court with the approval of such court;

(c) visit, under intimation to the State Government, any jail or any other institution under the control of the State Government, where persons are detained or lodged for purposes of treatment, reformation or protection to study the living conditions of the inmates and make recommendations thereon;

(d) review the safeguards provided by or under the Constitution or any law for the time being in force for the protection of human rights and recommend measures for their effective implementation;

(e) review the factors, including acts of terrorism, that inhibit the enjoyment of human rights and recommend appropriate remedial measures;

(f) study treaties and other international instruments on human rights and make recommendations for their effective implementation;

(g) undertake and promote research in the field of human rights;

(h) spread human rights literacy among various sections of society and promote awareness of the safeguards available for the protection of these rights through publications, the media, seminars and other available means;

(i) encourage the efforts of non-governmental organisations and institutions working in the field of human rights;

(j) such other functions as it may consider necessary for the protection of human rights.

13. Powers Relating to Inquiries

(1) The Commission shall, while inquiring into complaints under this Act, have all the powers of a civil court trying a suit under the Code of Civil Procedure, 1908, and in particular in respect of the following matters, namely:—

(a) summoning and enforcing the attendance of witnesses and examine them on oath;

(b) discovery and production of any document;

(c) receiving evidence on affidavits;

(d) requisitioning any public record or copy thereof from any court or office;

(e) issuing commissions for the examination of witnesses or documents;

(f) any other matter which may be prescribed.

(2) The Commission shall have power to require any person, subject to any privilege which may be claimed by that person under any law for the time being in force, to furnish information on such points or matters as, in the

opinion of the Commission, may be useful for, or relevant to, the subject matter of the inquiry and any person so required shall be deemed to be legally bound to furnish such information within the meaning of section 176 and section 177 of the Indian Penal Code.

(3) The Commission or any other officer, not below the rank of a Gazetted Officer, specially authorised in this behalf by the Commission may enter any building or place where the Commission has reason to believe that any document relating to the subject matter of the inquiry may be found, and may seize any such document or take extracts or copies therefrom subject to the provisions of section 100 of the Code of Criminal Procedure, 1973, in so far as it may be applicable.

(4) The Commission shall be deemed to be a civil court and when any offence as is described in section 175, section 178, section 179, section 180 or section 228 of the Indian Penal Code is committed in the view or presence of the Commission, the Commission may, after recording the facts constituting the offence and the statement of the accused as provided for in the Code of Criminal Procedure, 1973, forward the case to a Magistrate having jurisdiction to try the same and the Magistrate to whom any such case is forwarded shall proceed to hear the complaint against the accused as if the case has been forwarded to him under section 346 of the Code of Criminal Procedure, 1973.

(5) Every proceeding before the Commission shall be deemed to be a judicial proceeding within the meaning of sections 193 and 228, and for the purposes of section 196 of the Indian Penal Code, and the Commission shall be deemed to be a civil court for all the purposes of section 195 and Chapter XXVI of the Code of Criminal Procedure, 1973.

14. Investigation

(1) The Commission may, for the purpose of conducting any investigation pertaining to the inquiry, utilise the services of any officer or investigation agency of the

Central Government or any State Government with the concurrence of the Central Government or the State Government, as the case may be.

(2) For the purpose of investigating into any matter pertaining to the inquiry, any officer or agency whose services are utilised under sub-section (1) may, subject to the direction and control of the Commission.—

(a) summon and enforce the attendance of any person and examine him;

(b) require the discovery and production of any document; and

(c) requisition any public record or copy thereof from any office.

(3) The provisions of section 15 shall apply in relation to any statement made by a person before any officer or agency whose services are utilised under sub-section (1) as they apply in relation to any statement made by a person in the course of giving evidence before the Commission.

(4) The officer or agency whose services are utilised under sub-section (1) shall investigate into any matter pertaining to the inquiry and submit a report thereon to the Commission within such period as may be specified by the Commission in this behalf.

(5) The Commission shall satisfy itself about the correctness of the facts stated and the conclusion, if any, arrived at in the report submitted to it under sub-section (4) and for this purpose the Commission may make such inquiry (including the examination of the person or persons who conducted or assisted in the investigation) as it thinks fit.

15. Statement made by persons to the Commission

No statement made by a person in the course of giving evidence before the Commission shall subject him to, or be used against him in, any civil or criminal proceeding except a prosecution for giving false evidence by such statement:

Provided that the statement:

(a) is made in reply to the question which he is required by the Commission to answer; or

(b) is relevant to the subject matter of the inquiry.

16. Persons Likely to be Prejudicially Affected to be Heard

If, at any stage of the inquiry, the Commission—

(a) considers it necessary to inquire into the conduct of any person; or

(b) is of the opinion that the reputation of any person is likely to be prejudicially affected by the inquiry;

it shall give to that person a reasonable opportunity of being heard in the inquiry and to produce evidence in his defence:

Provided that nothing in this section shall apply where the credit of a witness is being impeached.

Chapter IV

PROCEDURE

17. Inquiry into complaints

The Commission while inquiring into the complaints of violations of human rights may—

(i) call for information or report from the Central Government or any State Government or any other authority or organisation subordinate thereto within such time as may be specified by it:

Provided that—

(a) if the information or report is not received within the time stipulated by the Commission, it may proceed to inquire into the complaint on its own;

(b) if, on receipt of information or report, the Commission is satisfied either that no further inquiry is required or that the required action has been initiated or taken by the concerned Government or authority, it may not proceed with the complaint and inform the complainant accordingly;

(ii) without prejudice to anything contained in clause (i), if it considers necessary, having regard to the nature of the complaint, initiate an inquiry.

18. Steps After Inquiry

The Commission may take any of the following steps upon the completion of an inquiry held under this Act namely:—

(1) where the inquiry discloses, the commission of violation of human rights or negligence in the prevention of violation of human rights by a public servant, it may recommend to the concerned Government or authority the initiation of proceedings for prosecution or such other action as the Commission may deem fit against the concerned person or persons;

(2) approach the Supreme Court or the High Court concerned for such directions, orders or writs as that Court may deem necessary;

(3) recommend to the concerned Government or authority for the grant of such immediate interim relief to the victim or the members of his family as the Commission may consider necessary;

(4) subject to the provisions of clause (5), provide a copy of the inquiry report to the petitioner or his representative;

(5) the Commission shall send a copy of its inquiry report together with its recommendations to the concerned Government or authority and the concerned Government or authority shall, within a period of one month, or such further time as the Commission may allow, forward its comments on the report, including the action taken or proposed to be taken thereon, to the Commission;

(6) the Commission shall publish its inquiry report together with the comments of the concerned Government or authority, if any, and the action taken or proposed to be taken by the concerned Government or authority on the recommendations of the Commission.

19. Procedure with respect to armed forces

(1) Notwithstanding anything contained in this Act, while dealing with complaints of violation of human rights by members of the armed forces, the Commission shall adopt the following procedure, namely:—

(a) it may, either on its own motion or on receipt of a petition, seek a report from the Central Government;

(b) after the receipt of the report, it may, either not proceed with the complaint or, as the case may be, make its recommendations to that Government.

(2) The Central Government shall inform the Commission of the action taken on the recommendations within three months or such further time as the Commission may allow.

(3) The Commission shall publish its report together with its recommendations made to the Central Government and the action taken by that Government on such recommendations.

(4) The Commission shall provide a copy of the report published under sub-section (3) to the petitioner or his representative.

20. Annual and special reports of the Commission

(1) The Commission shall submit an annual report to the Central Government and to the State Government concerned and may at any time submit special reports on any matter which, in its opinion, is of such urgency or importance that it should not be deferred till submission of the annual report.

(2) The Central Government and the State Government, as the case may be, shall cause the annual and special reports of the Commission to be laid before each House of Parliament or the State Legislature respectively, as the case may be, along with a memorandum of action taken or proposed to be taken on the recommendations of the Commission and the reasons for non-acceptance of the recommendations, if any.

Chapter V

STATE HUMAN RIGHTS COMMISSIONS

21. Constitution of State Human Rights Commissions

(1) A State Government may constitute a body to be known as the .... (name of the State) Human Rights Commission to exercise the powers conferred upon, and to perform the functions assigned to, a State Commission under this Chapter.

(2) The State Commission shall consist of—

(a) a Chairperson who has been a Chief Justice of a High Court;

(b) one Member who is, or has been, a Judge of a High Court;

(c) one Member who is, or has been, a district judge in that State;

(d) two Members to be appointed from amongst persons having knowledge of, or practical experience in, matters relating to human rights.

(3) There shall be a Secretary who shall be the Chief Executive Officer of the State Commission and shall exercise such powers and discharge such functions of the State Commission as it may delegate to him.

(4) The headquarters of the State Commission shall be at such place as the State Government may, by notification, specify.

(5) A State Commission may inquire into violation of human rights only in respect of matters relatable to any of the entries enumerated in List II and List III in the Seventh Schedule to the Constitution:

Provided that if any such matter is already being inquired into by the Commission or any other Commission duly constituted under any law for the time being in force, the State Commission shall not inquire into the said matter:

Provided further that in relation to the Jammu and Kashmir Human Rights Commission, this sub-section shall have effect as if for the words and figures "List II and List lll in the Seventh Schedule to the Constitution", the words and figures "List III in the Seventh Schedule to the Constitution as applicable to the State of Jammu and Kashmir and in respect of matters in relation to which the Legislature of that State has power to make laws" had been substituted.

22. Appointment of Chairperson and other Members of State Commission

(1) The Chairperson and other Members shall be appointed by the Governor by warrant under his hand and seal:

Provided that every appointment under this sub-section shall be made after obtaining the recommendation of a Committee consisting of—

(a) the Chief Minister —Chairperson;

(b) Speaker of the Legislative Assembly —Member;

(c) Minister in-charge of the Department of Home, in that State —Member;

(d) Leader of the Opposition in the Legislative Assembly —Member:

Provided further that where there is Legislative Council in a State, the Chairman of that Council and the Leader of the Opposition in that Council shall also be members of the Committee.

Provided also that no sitting Judge of a High Court or a sitting District Judge shall be appointed except after consultation with the Chief Justice of the High Court of the concerned State.

(2) No appointment of a Chairperson or a Member of the State Commission shall be invalid merely by reason of any vacancy in the Committee.

23. Removal of a Member of the State Commission

(1) Subject to the provisions of sub-section (2), the Chairperson or any other member of the State Commission shall only be removed from his office by order of the President on the ground of proved

misbehaviour or incapacity after the Supreme Court, on a reference being made to it by the President, has, on inquiry held in accordance with the procedure prescribed in that behalf by the Supreme Court, reported that the Chairperson or such other Member, as the case may be, ought on any such ground to be removed.

(2) Notwithstanding anything in sub-section (1), the President may by order remove from office the Chairperson or any other Member if the Chairperson or such other Member, as the case may be, –

(a) is adjudged an insolvent; or

(b) engages during his term of office in any paid employment outside the duties of his office; or

(c) is unfit to continue in office by reason of infirmity of mind or body; or

(d) is of unsound mind and stands so declared by a competent court; or

(e) is convicted and sentenced to imprisonment for an offence which in the opinion of the President involves moral turpitude.

24. Term of office of Members of the State Commission

(1) A person appointed as Chairperson shall hold office for a term of five years from the date on which he enters upon his office or until he attains the age of seventy years, whichever is earlier;

(2) A person appointed as a Member shall hold office for a term of five years from the date on which he enters upon his office and shall be eligible for re-appointment for another term of five years:

Provided that no Member shall hold office after he has attained the age of seventy years.

(3) On ceasing to hold office, a Chairperson or a Member shall be ineligible for further employment under the Government of a State or under the Government of India.

25. Member to act as Chairperson or to discharge his functions in certain circumstances

(1) In the event of the occurrence of any vacancy in the office of the Chairperson by reason of his death, resignation or otherwise, the Governor may, by notification, authorise one of the Members to act as the Chairperson until the appointment of a new Chairperson to fill such vacancy.

(2) When the Chairperson is unable to discharge his functions owing to absence on leave or otherwise, such one of the Members as the Governor may, by notification, authorise in this behalf, shall discharge the functions of the Chairperson until the date on which the Chairperson resumes his duties.

26. Terms and conditions of service of Members of the State Commission

The salaries and allowances payable to, and other terms and conditions of service of, the Members shall be such as may be prescribed by the State Government:

Provided that neither the salary and allowances nor the other terms and conditions of service of a Member shall be varied to his disadvantage after his appointment.

27. Officers and other staff of the State Commission

(1) The State Government shall make available to the Commission—

(a) an officer not below the rank of a Secretary to the State Government who shall be the Secretary of the State Commission; and

(b) such police and investigative staff under an officer not below the rank of an Inspector General of Police and such other officers and staff as may be necessary for the efficient performance of the functions of the State Commission.

(2) Subject to such rules as may be made by the State Government in this behalf, the State Commission may appoint such other administrative, technical and scientific staff as it may consider necessary.

(3) The salaries, allowances and conditions of service of the officers and other staff appointed under sub-section (2) shall be such as may be prescribed by the State Government.

28. Annual and special reports of State Commission

(1) The State Commission shall submit an annual report to the State Government and may at any time submit special reports on any matter which, in its opinion, is of such urgency or importance that it should not be deferred till submission of the annual report.

(2) The State Government shall cause the annual and special reports of the State Commission to be laid before each House of State Legislature where it consists of two Houses, or where such Legislature consists of one House, before that House along with a memorandum of action taken or proposed to be taken on the recommendations of the State Commission and the reasons for non-acceptance of the recommendations, if any.

29. Application of certain Provisions Relating to National Human Rights Commission to State Commissions

The provisions of sections 9, 10, 12, 13, 14, 15, 16, 17 and 18 shall apply to a State Commission and shall have effect, subject to the following modifications, namely:—

(a) references to "Commission" shall be construed as references to "State Commission";

(b) in section 10, in sub-section (3), for the word "Secretary General", the word "Secretary" shall be substituted;

(c) in section 12, clause (f) shall be omitted;

(d) in section 17, in clause (i), the words "Central Government or any" shall be omitted.

Chapter VI

HUMAN RIGHTS COURTS

30. Human Right Courts

For the purpose of providing speedy trial of offences arising out of violation of human rights, the State Government may, with the concurrence of the Chief Justice of the High Court, by notification, specify for each district a Court of Session to be a Human Rights Court to try the said offences:

Provided that nothing in this section shall apply, if —

(a) a Court of Session is already specified as a special court; or

(b) a special court is already constituted,

for such offences under any other law for the time being in force.

31. Special Public Prosecutor

For every Human Rights Court, the State Government shall, by notification, specify a Public Prosecutor or appoint an advocate who has been in practice as an advocate for not less than seven years, as a Special Public Prosecutor for the purpose of conducting cases in that Court.

Chapter VII

FINANCE, ACCOUNTS AND AUDIT

32. Grants by the Central Government

(1) The Central Government shall, after due appropriation made by Parliament by law in this behalf, pay to the Commission by way of grants such sums of money as the Central Government may think fit for being utilised for the purposes of this Act.

(2) The Commission may spend such sums as it thinks fit for performing the functions under this Act, and such sums shall be treated as expenditure payable out of the grants referred to in sub-section (1).

33. Grants by the State Government

(1) The State Government shall, after due appropriation made by Legislature by law in this behalf, pay to the State Commission by way of grants such sums of money as the State Government may think fit for being utilised for the purposes of this Act.

(2) The State Commission may spend such sums as it thinks fit for performing the functions under Chapter V, and

such sums shall be treated as expenditure payable out of the grants referred to in sub-section (1).

34. Accounts and Audit

(1) The Commission shall maintain proper accounts and other relevant records and prepare an annual statement of accounts in such form as may be prescribed by the Central Government in consultation with the Comptroller and Auditor-General of India.

(2) The Accounts of the Commission shall be audited by the Comptroller and Auditor-General at such intervals as may be specified by him and any expenditure incurred in connection with such audit shall be payable by the Commission to the Comptroller and Auditor-General.

(3) The Comptroller and Auditor-General, and any person appointed by him in connection with the audit of the accounts of the Commission under this Act shall have the same rights and privileges and the authority in connection with such audit as the Comptroller and Auditor-General generally has in connection with the audit of Government accounts and, in particular, shall have the right to demand the production of books, accounts, connected vouchers and other documents and papers and to inspect any of the offices of the Commission.

(4) The accounts of the Commission, as certified by the Comptroller and Auditor-General or any other person appointed by him in this behalf, together with the audit report thereon, shall be forwarded only to the Central Government by the Commission and the Central Government shall cause the audit report to be laid, as soon as may be after it is received, before each House of Parliament.

35. Accounts and Audit of State Commission

(1) The State Commission shall maintain proper accounts and other relevant records and prepare an annual statement of accounts in such form as may be prescribed by the State Government in consultation with the Comptroller and Auditor-General of India.

(2) The accounts of the State Commission shall be audited by the Comptroller and Auditor-General at such intervals as may be specified by him and any expenditure incurred in connection with such audit shall be payable by the State Commission to the Comptroller and Auditor-General.

(3) The Comptroller and Auditor-General, and any person appointed by him in connection with the audit of the accounts of the State Commission under this Act shall have the same rights and privileges and the authority in connection with such audit as the Comptroller and Auditor-General generally has in connection with the audit of Government accounts and, in particular, shall have the right to demand the production of books, accounts, connected vouchers and other documents and papers and to inspect any of the offices of the State Commission.

(4) The accounts of the State Commission, as certified by the Comptroller and Auditor-General or any other person appointed by him in this behalf, together with the audit report thereon, shall be forwarded annually to the State Government by the State Commission and the State Government shall cause the audit report to be laid, as soon as may be after it is received, before the State Legislature.

Chapter VIII

MISCELLANEOUS

36. Matters not subject to jurisdiction of the Commission

(1) The Commission shall not inquire into any matter which is pending before a State Commission or any other Commission duly constituted under any law for the time being in force.

(2) The Commission or the State Commission shall not inquire into any matter after the expiry of one year from the date on which the act constituting violation of human rights is alleged to have been committed.

37. Constitution of special investigation teams

Notwithstanding anything contained in any other law for the time being in force, where the Government considers it necessary so to do, it may constitute one or more special investigation teams, consisting of such police officers as it thinks necessary for purposes of investigation and prosecution of offences arising out of violations of human rights.

38. Protection of action taken in good faith

No suit or other legal proceeding shall lie against the Central Government, State Government, Commission, the State Commission or any Member thereof or any person acting under the direction either of the Central Government, State Government, Commission or the State Commission in respect of anything which is in good faith done or intended to be done in pursuance of this Act or of any rules or any order made thereunder or in respect of the publication by or under the authority of the Central Government, State Government, Commission or the State Commission of any report, paper or proceedings.

39. Members and officers to be public servants

Every Member of the Commission, State Commission and every officer appointed or authorised by the Commission or the State Commission to exercise functions under this Act shall be deemed to be a public servant within the meaning of section 21 of the Indian Penal Code.

40. Power of Central Government to make rules

(1) The Central Government may, by notification, make rules to carry out the provisions of this Act.

(2) In particular and without prejudice to the generality of the foregoing power, such rules may provide for all or any of the following matters namely:—

(a) the salaries and allowances and other terms and conditions of service of the Members under section 8;

(b) the conditions subject to which other administrative, technical and scientific staff may be appointed by the Commission and the salaries and allowances of officers and other staff under sub-section (3) of section 11;

(c) any other power of a civil court required to be prescribed under clause (f) of sub-section (1) of section .13;

(d) the form in which the annual statement of accounts is to be pre pared by the Commission under sub-section (1) of section 34; and

(e) any other matter which has to be, or may be, prescribed.

(3) Every rule made under this Act shall be laid, as soon as may be after it is made, before each House of Parliament, while it is in session, for a total period of thirty days which may be comprised in one session or in two or more successive sessions, and if, before the expiry of the session immediately following the session or the successive sessions aforesaid, both Houses agree in making any modification in the rule or both Houses agree that the rule should not be made, the rule shall thereafter have effect only in such modified form or be of no effect, as the case may be; so, however, that any such modification or annulment shall be without prejudice to the validity of anything previously done under that rule.

41. Power of State Government to make rules

(1) The State Government may, by notification, make rules to carry out the provisions of this Act.

(2) In particular and without prejudice to the generality of the fore going power, such rules may provide for all or any of the following matters, namely:—

(a) the salaries and allowances and other terms and conditions of service of the Members under section 26;

(b) the conditions subject to which other administrative, technical and scientific staff may be appointed by the State Commission and the salaries and allowances of officers and other staff under sub-section (3) of section 27;

(c) the form in which the annual statement of accounts is to be prepared under sub-section (1) of section 35.

(3) Every rule made by the State Government under this section shall be laid, as soon as may be after it is made, before each House of the State Legislature where it consists of two Houses, or where such Legislature consists of one House, before that House.

42. Power to remove difficulties

(1) If any difficulty arises in giving effect to the provisions of this Act, the Central Government may, by order published in the Official Gazette, make such provisions, not inconsistent with the provisions of this Act as appear to it to be necessary or expedient for removing the difficulty:

Provided that no such order shall be made after the expiry of the period of two years from the date of commencement of this Act.

(2) Every order made under this section shall, as soon as may be after it is made, be laid before each house of Parliament.

43. Repeal and Savings

(1) The Protection of Human Rights Ordinance, 1993 is hereby repealed.

(2) Notwithstanding such repeal, anything done or any action taken under the said Ordinance, shall be deemed to have been done or taken under the corresponding provisions of this Act.

Index